Friendship: The Key to Spiritual Growth

John W. Crossin, O.S.F.S.

Paulist Press ✦ New York ✦ Mahwah, N.J.

Library of Congress Cataloging-in-Publication Data

Crossin, John W.
   Friendship : the key to spiritual growth / John W. Crossin.
     p. cm.
   Includes bibliographical references and index.
   ISBN 0-8091-3710-0 (alk. paper)
   1. Spiritual life—Catholic Church.   2. Friendship—Religious aspects—Christianity. 3. Catholic Church—Doctrines. I. Title.
BX2350.2.C76 1997
241'.6762—dc21   97-6425
                                                     CIP

Published by Paulist Press
997 Macarthur Boulevard
Mahwah, New Jersey 07430

Printed and bound in the
United States of America

Contents

I am happy to dedicate this book to my four friends:
Kevin Barry
Sheila Garcia
Elizabeth Le Buffe
Rowena Muller Morris

Acknowledgments

This book reflects the collaborative efforts of many people. I dedicate it to my friends in the **De Sales Group**, Kevin Barry, Sheila Garcia, Betty Le Buffe and Rowena Muller Morris. Our continuing discussions over many years encouraged me to write. Their critical analysis, suggestions and support have enabled me to clarify and develop the thoughts contained herein.

I also owe a debt of gratitude to Richard Reece, O.S.F.S., the former Provincial of the Oblates of St. Francis de Sales of the Wilmington-Philadelphia Province. He encouraged my writing and provided a summer sabbatical where much of the groundwork for this volume and its companion was laid. My fellow Oblates at Deshairs House, De Sales School of Theology and Bishop Ireton High School (site of my summer sabbatical) have also been most supportive of me as I pursued this work in their midst.

Many people have commented on outlines and drafts of this work. These friendly commentators included Jerry Bench, Pat and Ed Grenier, Jerry John, Tim Nolan, Lucille Emily, Ron Selzer, John Weiland and David and Kathleen Woodward. My students in my courses on Friendship and on Collaborative Ministry have also been very helpful with their discussion of some of these ideas. I am most grateful to them.

I also offer my thanks to those who so willingly gave permission to me to use work first published by them:

To the United States Catholic Conference for the article "Friendship: Key to Growth in Virtue," which appeared in *The Living Light,* vol. 32, no. 4, Summer, 1996, and offers an overview of much of the present work.

To the *Deacon Digest* for the articles on "Spiritual Progress" and "Healing," which appeared in the digest in February and August, 1991, and reappear (in part) in Chapters 2 and 7, respectively.

To the Catholic News Service for permission to use part of the article "How Do You Spell V-I-R-T-U-E" from the *Faith Alive* series in Chapter 8.

The two excerpts from the poetry of Jessica Powers in Chapter 5, the first from "This Trackless Solitude" and the second from "If You Have Nothing," are reprinted with permission of Sheed & Ward, 115 E. Armour Blvd., Kansas City, MO 64111. To order, call (800) 333-7373.

Introduction

The search for spiritual meaning grips Americans today. We are asking questions such as: Where am I headed? What am I searching for? What will my life contribute? What are my priorities?

These are very personal questions. They focus on the individual and his or her fulfillment and are signs of experience and mature reflection on life. Yet they miss the fact that we do not and cannot define ourselves alone. Our relationships with others make us who we are. Our deepest questions are only answerable in dialogue with others. Friendships are the key to our spiritual growth.

From the beginning, our relationship with our mother in the womb formed us. We grew to maturity in and through relationships with parents, family and friends. If these were not present and positive, then we may very well have developed personal deficiencies and even have been involved in personal disasters.

In this book I affirm that friendships spur us to spiritual growth. Our quest for meaning intimately involves friendship—with self, others and God. These relationships anchor our spiritual life and set our priorities. Friendships flourish within the supportive context of communities. Religious and civil communities and small "intentional" groups are absolutely necessary for our friendships to thrive. They

1

give us substance and direction and help us to stay focused on what is most important.

Spiritual and moral growth are necessarily intertwined. We don't have one without the other. Personal spiritual growth inevitably involves reaching out to others and making wise and loving moral decisions that form our character, making us certain kinds of persons. I hope to explore the development of Christian character in more depth in a companion volume that will build on the present work.

My purpose in this book is to speak to others who are asking questions about the spiritual meaning of life. I hope to do so in practical ways, out of the Catholic tradition and with an emphasis on the spiritual teachings of St. Francis de Sales (1567–1622) and St. Jane de Chantal (1572–1641). As a young man I encountered their practical spiritual wisdom, and to this day I find their emphasis on the commonsense virtues of daily living essential for my spiritual life. I hope that my reflections, grounded in a wise spiritual tradition, may be helpful to all those seeking their own spiritual growth.

These reflections rest on a long tradition of virtue-centered thinking in Christianity. Nowadays, even the national political discussion has come around to addressing such topics as the importance of character, living a virtuous life, good example, community and the common good. Business leaders are urged to develop character and personal integrity to achieve long-term success.

From my point of view, growth in virtue is the substance of the spiritual life. While it is true that virtues are chosen personally, they are formed in relationships with others.

I present the ideas here in summary form—practical issues more for purposes of illustration than for exhaustive analysis. I hope that my ideas will be accessible to busy people and be a source of personal reflection and growth.

The chapters are short so that they might be easily considered by readers who have limited time. The questions are to aid personal reflection and to encourage sharing with others.

Ultimately, friendship, community, spiritual growth and moral growth go together. Our project is to explore their connections as we seek to make sense out of our lives.

I. The World Today[1]

The state of the world around us is really the state of ourselves—for American culture is not only around us, it is *in* us. Depending on our generation and the particular location and circumstances of our life's journey, we have taken in a greater or smaller amount of American values and priorities. While we can be critical of our culture, we are also part of it. And it deeply affects our spiritual life.

These days we seem to be a culture in transition. The future is not at all clear and the high hopes of the so-called baby-boom generation of the 1960s, of which I am a member, have been, if not dashed, at least greatly sobered.

Violence seems to surround us. Local and national news programs bring us up-to-date on the latest murders and bombings. Friends tell us of the violence—physical or verbal—they have experienced. Movies and music add to our sense of the pervasiveness and acceptability of violence toward others. If we happen to be called to jury duty, we may very well find ourselves judging a case where a shooting or other mayhem grew out of the drug trade. The witnesses provide an inside look at the lack of norms and moral breakdown that pervade certain segments of society. For example, in a recent case the defendant contended that he couldn't have done the shooting because he was at home in bed with "the mother of his child." She is not his wife.

A related cause for concern is the rootlessness of people. Some of us move around frequently and thus do not have the joys and constraints that come from being part of a set community with consistent relationships. Add to this the rise of the single-parent family with the predominant absence of fathers, and we have a social situation where the transmission of moral principles and the constraints on violence often are diminished.

These persistent signs point to the change we have experienced, part of which over the last thirty years has been our move away from prayer and the spiritual life. I am convinced that our relationship with God is vitally important for our lives. The absence of a living faith in God is one root of our distress.

Psychological Conditioning

Often these days our culture puts its faith in psychological ideas and systems involving conditioning, repression and denial. Psychological theories are widely espoused in which most of the things we do come from the influence of our environment or because of the way our parents treated us in childhood. God is but a projection of our inner fears and insecurities, or our belief in God is the result of social conditioning.

Many summers ago, when studying for a master's degree in psychology, I came to the realization that psychology was the belief system of some of my fellow students. It wasn't just a tool as it was for me; it was the toolbox. For them, all earthly and heavenly events could be explained by conditioning, repression and various other psychological concepts. I found this faith in Freud or other psychologists curious. What I was learning was that the various psychological theories didn't agree with each other, they varied greatly in their understanding of human nature and were sometimes at completely opposite poles in their explanations. Material we studied showed that one school of thought seemed just as effective as another when it came to getting good results in therapy. And just as many people recovered from their problems without any counseling.

The dominant popular psychological approaches focused on self-fulfillment and self-development with an emphasis on personal freedom. The tone was subjective. At times, it seemed as if other people existed merely to fulfill the needs of the individual or to be blamed for personal problems or shortcomings. This approach manifested itself in the sexual revolution of the 1960s and later in the so-called me decade of the 1980s.

The longer we live, the more we see that most of our actions are our responsibility and that there is an objective world beyond our subjectivity and personal fulfillment. Psychological models have some validity but they certainly don't explain the meaning of life. As one psychologist argues:

> ...therapists since the time of Freud have overemphasized individual self-interest, giving short shrift to family and community responsibilities. [This book] calls for the inclusion of moral discourse in the practice of psychotherapy and the cultivation in therapists of the virtues and skills needed to be moral consultants to their clients....[2]

Therapeutic models, while helpful, are far from comprehensive and are legitimately open to question. I believe that morality, severed from its relationship to God and the spiritual life, is essentially rootless and will not ultimately be taken seriously by students or clients in therapy. Conversion and spiritual growth motivate moral decisions.

Teaching programs designed to instill ethical conduct—whether in individual therapy, in high schools or in business schools—will fail unless rooted in spiritual realities such as conversion and commitment.

I believe that it is no accident that the breakdown of the family and the disturbing social trends toward illegitimacy, drug abuse and other widely documented social evils[3] have occurred at a time when self-fulfillment is exalted and standards are dismissed as old fashioned. Problems have increased so much that the rate of breakdown of the black family decried by Daniel Moynihan in the 1960s is now the rate of breakdown of the white family in the 1990s.

These social trends are now leading to a reconsideration of our moral stance. The sexual revolution was a great success. Its tenets of individual expressiveness are the norm today. Yet it has become apparent that this norm is seriously flawed. As Barbara Dafoe Whitehead noted in *The Atlantic:*

> After decades of public dispute about so-called family diversity, the evidence from social-science research is coming in: The dissolution of two-parent families, though it may benefit the adults involved, is harmful to many children, and dramatically undermines our society.[4]

As Senator Moynihan has noted, by "defining deviancy down,"[5] we legitimize what was once seen as abnormal behavior. Thus violence, single parenthood and cohabitation are acceptable. Moreover, in an era of sexual expressiveness and lack of restraint, it comes as no surprise that rape and abuse seem to be more common.

The Turn to Values

We have experienced a shift from external and objective norms to personal preferences and individual self-interest.

In recent decades, we have moved from virtues to values. Values are subjective and personal; virtues relate us to standards. Values emphasize personal expression; virtues call us to self-discipline.

The turn to values is of recent origin. It started most clearly in the last century with the philosopher Friedrich Nietzsche, who severed the relationship of values from truth. "'Values' brought with it the assumption that all moral ideas are subjective and relative...they can be beliefs, opinions, attitudes, feelings, habits, conventions, preferences, prejudices, even idiosyncrasies...."[6] At the same time, moral language changed from terms such as *bad* or *sinful* to *undesirable* or *inappropriate*.

In contrast, the virtues of many previous generations had deep roots in religion and in their sense of community. The self was known to be for others. As this customary morality waned in our century, and was replaced by a secular agnosticism, the virtues were replaced by values.

The emphasis on values reflects our tendency to stress the individual over the community. We are an individualistic culture; we emphasize rights over responsibilities. As Robert Bellah and his colleagues noted some years ago:

> What has failed at every level—from the society of nations to the national society to the local community to the family—is integration: we have failed to remember "our community as members of the same body," as John Winthrop put it. We have committed what to the republican founders of our nation was the cardinal sin: we have put our own good, as individuals, as groups, as a nation, ahead of the common good.[7]

In previous eras, the commitment of individuals to moral principles and the power of social institutions such as churches mitigated the excesses of individualism.

Unfortunately, this is not the case today as Christian believers seek to build communities that will work to change the cultural norm rather than to support it.

Belief in Science

If psychology or personal values is the real credo of many people today, science is the faith of others. Years ago, as a young person attracted to the study of mathematics, I used to wonder if science and its great advances in our time could explain everything. Recently however, some scientists have become humble—admitting that finding cures can be an arduous process (e.g., for AIDS); that they operate out of somewhat limited paradigms; that science is no substitute for moral integrity (e.g., in using nuclear weapons); and that they cannot explain all of reality, including ultimate things.

Science is a wonderful tool, but it does not provide ultimate meaning. The person who is searching spiritually pays careful attention to the findings of physics and biology but realizes that human reality extends beyond their limited scope.

Pursuit of Pleasure

More practically, perhaps we've put our confidence not in science or psychology or values but in the pursuit of pleasure—the theme of so much of our modern music and the underlying message of advertising (after all, we do deserve only the best!). Yet we've learned from experience that pleasure is not happiness and does not give life meaning. Pleasure diverts us but does not answer our ultimate questions.

We may be like the woman who said:

I found myself crying. I sat in my beautiful new house with the lights off thinking. I had thought this would make me happy…as soon as I had this car or this house or whatever it was, then I'd be happy. But I looked at all I had and I wasn't anything I wanted to be.[8]

One characteristic value of contemporary American society is greed—for money, power, recognition or knowledge. We see this in the financial excesses on Wall Street and in professional sports. Or, more mundanely, we see it in our purchase of items we rarely use or books we never read. One acquaintance of mine decided that from now on he would not buy a new book until he finished reading the one he had bought previously. This change not only saved him money but made him more conscious of his inability to know or do everything he would like. In seeking to have many things, we can wind up having nothing substantive.

Material goods, personal preference, psychology and science, each valid in its own domain, leave us with a tinge of skepticism and no practical belief. We become skilled in critiquing others, but less so in offering a positive vision of life. Just like many involved in contemporary politics, we can be more adept at the negative campaign—in pointing out the faults of others—than in building a positive future. It is only when we become dissatisfied with negativity, however, that we may eventually begin to search for more substance for our lives.

Signs of Hope

"We must first study the shadows if we are to paint the light." This remark by an art student to a colleague of mine applies to our project as well. We first look at the darkness—both inside and around us—in order to move toward the good of friendship. If insecurity, greed, violence, sexual license, family and community breakdown and excessive individualism are readily observable characteristics of our culture, so too are more positive trends.

Having conceded the difficulties and distractions that confront us daily, we might give more than equal time to some of the hopeful signs around us that promise support and encouragement for our growth in the spiritual life. Progress is made, after all, not by those who eternally lament what is wrong, but by those who choose to focus on what is right and dare to build a life of hope. The hope I speak of is a virtue essential to the spiritual life. It is a hope not born of wishful thinking or baseless optimism but rather founded on God's promise to be with us always. There are rays of sun peeking out from behind the clouds that indicate a resurgence in the strength of people's desire to reach out to others and to God. We will consider a few examples, some drawing national attention, others from personal experience.

Searching for Community

People today are searching for community in what they frequently perceive as a rather impersonal world. Whether in a twelve-step program, neighborhood group or bible study, we need the warmth of human interaction and sharing face to face. Many of us belong to such small "intentional groups," which are the fastest growing movement in America today. In a survey completed in 1991 by the Gallup Institute involving 1,900 randomly chosen Americans, 40 percent of those responding said that they participate in small groups, two-thirds of which have a religious orientation. This is a new phenomenon that is being hailed as the wave of the future, possibly even the future of the churches.[9] It would seem that we are clearly growing more conscious of our need and desire to make time for the spiritual.

Small faith communities, whether independent or attached to local churches, are offering spiritual sustenance to their members by combining prayer, continued learning and support for each other with the social missions they undertake. Whatever they accomplish for the common good, small groups also give their members a network of supportive and caring friends, enabling members to make connections that might not have been possible otherwise.

As members of small groups, we need to challenge ourselves to become more focused on the common good of society. Participation in community can make demands on us that call us to spiritual maturity. A Christian community's demand for truthfulness, for example, can call into question some of our business practices and our rationalization of them. The community's standards can challenge us to greater truthfulness and integrity in our dealings with others.

A second sign of hope is the shift in part of the business community from an approach based on personality to one based on character. This shift is important, though its implementation is far from universal. Stephen R. Covey advocates this approach in his influential book *The 7 Habits of Highly Effective People.*[10] He argues for principles, not merely values:

> The Character Ethic is based on the fundamental idea that there are *principles* that govern human effectiveness—natural laws in the human dimension that are just as real, just as unchanging and unarguably "there" as laws such as gravity are in the physical dimension.[11]

Principles such as fairness, trust, integrity, honesty, service, quality, potential and growth are the deep truths of humanity and should form our actions. Business practices rooted deeply in human character are the ones that succeed in the long run. Covey argues comprehensively for business practices that conform to the deeper levels of our humanity.

If Covey argues for a character-grounded approach to effective leadership in business, William Bennett does the same for the education of children in *The Book of Virtues,* which became an unexpected best-seller.[12] The book is a compilation of traditional stories, poems, myths and other tales of virtuous conduct. Bennett believes that we learn by example and seeks "to show parents, teachers, students, and children what the virtues look like, what they are in practice, how to recognize them and how they work."[13] He believes that such examples provide specific "moorings" in life that help us all come to maturity. The stories are such that some of them can be read to children at bedtime. Yet they are so many and diverse that they can provide a good study for adults as well.

A further sign of hope is the reemergence of religion in the public forum. In recent decades, religious institutions and principles have been pushed from the public square—especially from the media—by a growing secularization and by the belief that religion is a private matter, resting in emotion. Only prominent international religious figures, such as the pope, and powerful political forces, such as the Christian Coalition, are given much hearing. Rare is the religious figure—Catholic, Protestant, Jewish or Muslim—who would be interviewed in any depth, for example, on a Sunday morning news program.

Some signs indicate that this situation is coming a bit more into balance. Both the questioning of the dominant role of the social and the hard sciences, and the failure of secular solutions to stem the forces of violence and social disintegration have led to a renewed interest in the role of religious institutions in the broader society. This manifests itself in more frequent media interviews with religious people—especially those engaged in the works of mercy. There is human interest in the charitable practices that upbuild the community such as the works of the Missionaries of Charity founded by Mother Teresa. A next step should be the reappearance of discourse by religious people in the public square. There can and should be room for religious people to be heard on the great issues of our time.

The emergence of small communities, the advocacy of principle-centered business practices, the renewal of education in virtue and the rising awareness of the importance of religion are signs of hope for a renewal of our civil and religious communities. In addition, we are aware that organizations like "Christmas in April" have grown over a decade from rebuilding a few homes for the needy in one city to rebuilding tens of thousands a year, all with donated services from caring people—many of whom don't pick up a paintbrush at any other time of the year!

On a more personal level, each of us knows someone who makes time every week to visit the elderly in the hospital, or AIDS patients in a hospice, or the bereaved at home, bringing the love and prayers of their community. The signs of hope are evident around us.

We carry around in us both signs of hope and of despair. Violence is not just outside us but in us. We have angry and vengeful thoughts that manifest themselves in rude behavior, verbal abuse, aggressive driving and in other individual ways. But we also feel compassion and engage in caring for others. We yearn to be part of something bigger than ourselves, to connect with something that gives meaning and purpose to our existence. While we may be able to do little to change the world, we can change ourselves—and that may lead, in time, to change in our local environments.

Commitment

Thirty years ago I joined a Catholic religious community, the Oblates of St. Francis de Sales. I had made a major decision and moved to a different state and met a new group of people. The first six weeks were a wonderful spiritual experience as I felt that joy, peace and consolation in prayer I had always wanted. Unfortunately, these feelings did not last. I returned to normal and eventually experienced those doubts and second thoughts that are a part of the spiritual journey.

I learned that to grow spiritually I would need to make a long-term commitment, and work my way through the inevitable ups and downs of life. Such knowledge did not come easily, and I have come to see that there are no shortcuts. If the signs of hope are to be sustained and developed, I will have to work at them persistently and with the help of others.

To change ourselves and our environments we need to make commitments—to a spouse, to children, to a vocation, to the community, to our friends. Essentially, we need to be persons of *commitment* who keep commitments.[14] Why make commitments? Or why keep them? What keeps us from making them? "Baby boomers" like myself, schooled in contemporary skepticism, have trouble firmly pledging ourselves to almost anything. Our trust level is low and often we are suspicious of others and their motivation. We would rather be in isolation than take the risks associated with commitments and change.

We "boomers" also tend to confuse "what I want" with "what I truly need." The affluent society that allows for extended education and material comfort transforms our passing desires into inner imperatives which must be fulfilled. A sense of sacrifice and limitation (we can't have everything) becomes more distant. While our parents and grandparents might have waited for decades for material comforts, we want them immediately. Instead of leaving behind the selfishness of youth where we had to be taught to share, we have instead developed a more sophisticated selfishness. In so doing we have distanced ourselves from the rigors of commitments.

A few years ago on a trip to Romania I met a Greek-Catholic priest, who had a white beard, wore a black cassock, and had a certain mystical look in his eyes. He had been in prison for seventeen years. Yet, he had survived to continue his work. A crowd comes to his daily mass. Here was a man of commitment who was still working hard for things that really mattered. How many skeptics go to prison?

How is it that he is a man of commitment and we are tinged with skepticism? Perhaps he's a relic of times gone by. Or perhaps we are encumbered by a way of thinking that does not make for lasting happiness.

Commitments call us *to go deeper*. They call us deeper within—beyond the roots of action to the roots of our being. What are we here for? What is most worth doing and what is secondary?

Commitment *calls us out of ourselves* to deeper relationships with others. It is not easy. A solid commitment to relationships and to community takes time and sacrifice and the patience to endure failure. To make commitments and keep them we need the support of others. Even then, they are difficult! Friends cannot substitute for personal generosity and moral courage.

In the end skepticism is inadequate. It is only in taking personal responsibility and seeking to transform our environment for the good that we will be happy. Commitments to others and their well being can make us whole. But to keep such commitments we need to develop virtues— ways of acting that integrate our clearest understandings and our deepest feelings as we reach out toward others.We will begin now to consider the essential elements of spiritual growth.

QUESTIONS FOR REFLECTION AND DISCUSSION

1. How do your beliefs, habits and attitudes reflect the American culture that surrounds us?

2. What is your perception of the state of our American culture?

3. Have you ever belonged to a small group? What were the benefits and drawbacks of membership?

4. What are your commitments and priorities? How are you trying to keep them?

II. Growing Spiritually

I have known a few people who have a deep inner peace-fulness. They radiate a certain tranquility and a deep spiri-tuality. When I am visiting these friends, peace seems to spread from them to me in a gentle way. For the next twenty-four hours or so I share in this peace. But then it disappears and I return to normal.

I believe that such inner peace and joy is the fruit of spir-itual growth and flows from commitment to positive rela-tionships, to friendships. In classical terms, this spiritual growth is growth in virtue—in doing the good and thereby becoming a better person. Many people today still think of their spiritual lives as obeying the law rather than as grow-ing in virtue. This legal approach has been dominant for decades, if not centuries, and is not without merit.

To know and live the moral law, as stated in the Ten Commandments for instance, is absolutely necessary. We would sleep better at night if we knew that the other mem-bers of our civic community were committed to abiding by the Ten Commandments. A common commitment to moral law is essential if society is to be peaceable and just. Moral norms are necessary for weak creatures who struggle at times to attain the minimum of human decency. We need the prohibitions against lying, stealing, cheating, adultery, and so forth, because we all are tempted at times, some of us frequently. The law can bring us face to face with our immoral patterns of acting. But we know that the law is the minimum; it is the boundary. What is more important in the spiritual life is growth beyond the minimum. This is growth in virtue.

If we consult the classical tradition, we might say that growth in virtue enables us to attain the fullest potentials of our human nature.[1] By living virtuously—that is, justly, humbly, prudently, faithfully and so forth—a person comes to perfection, or at least as near to it as one can in this life. Virtues are "traits of character needed 'for living well the sort of life that is characteristic of human beings.'"[2]

Virtues make for human happiness. Robert Hutchins, then president of the University of Chicago, noted years ago that just as virtue makes our work good, so also it makes us happy, for "happiness is activity in accordance with virtue."[3] We do not aim directly at happiness. Rather, in living purposefully, we become happy. We come to be at peace with ourselves. Happiness is not a moment-by-moment thing but rather the positive fruit of disciplined living.

How might we grow spiritually? How do we attain the virtues? We do so first of all by taking responsibility for ourselves and deciding to become virtuous people, which is much more easily said than done. Taking responsibility may be difficult since we may not know ourselves well enough or even recognize our patterns of acting. Developing a heightened sense of responsibility makes it tougher to blame "a system," or our past for who we are and what we do. It can be convenient to blame the boss, the government, our spouse, the pastor or some authority figure rather than to examine ourselves. This is not to say that there are not influences on our behavior, or that others are not ever at fault. But we can presume that we are the primary determiners of our character. As we come to know ourselves better, we can see our patterns of acting more clearly and choose to continue them or begin to change them.

If we are the primary developers of our own character, if we are basically responsible for our own spiritual growth, then we have to make some decisions. We have to set a direction or a renewed direction. We have to decide that we want to continue more intensely on the spiritual journey. Initially, one of the things we have to decide to do is to listen to our inner selves, to others, to our environment and to God, for we always have much to learn.

To Hear God, We Must Listen

Listening is an important part of the Christian tradition. The Virgin Mary listened to Gabriel, the shepherds, Simeon, Anna and her son Jesus. While Martha labored, Mary sat listening at Jesus' feet. The saints listen to God and then seek God's special call to them. Real happiness comes from hearing the word of God and putting it into practice.

Listening takes us out of ourselves. God speaks to us personally in a variety of ways—in scripture, in the tradition, through physical nature and human nature, through our friends and acquaintances, in our hearts—and thus we need to be attentive. We bring our whole being, seeing, hearing, sensing and feeling to the process. The fullness of life comes not just from within but from without.

St. Francis de Sales and St. Vincent de Paul (1581–1660) urge us to listen to everyone. Our superiors, equals, subordinates and especially the poor have something to say to us. God's truth is found on a variety of lips! Even people whom we deem to be somewhat odd may have something to say to us![4]

Each Christian institution seems to come complete with a few eccentrics. We can learn a lot from such seemingly foolish people. While much contemporary spiritual literature focuses on "development of self-esteem, inner healing or enhanced relationships,"[5] the weak and the gospel itself remind us that the spiritual life may involve pain and tumult. In the people from the halfway house or the drug rehabilitation center, in the fellow parishioner who asks a thousand questions or sings much too loudly, God may be speaking very directly to us.

Eccentricities are not confined to others. In our own personal foolishness and weakness, we can encounter God. "God lives and moves and has being in the entirety of the human condition, and most especially in what is lost, forgotten, despised, or cast aside."[6] Sometimes it is when we recognize the inadequacy of our own resources or even hit bottom that we become free to listen to God.

Obstacles to Listening

Listening is important but often hard to do. In the modern world, we are surrounded by noise and distractions that impede our listening. Just think of the background music in department stores or the constant blaring of radios and televisions that we tend to ignore. All this noise makes it hard to listen. I realized this years ago when I moved into a room right across the street from the church's bell tower. The bells chimed every fifteen minutes in a tone that could have wakened the dead. I thought that they would drive me crazy. But after two days I never heard them again. I automatically blocked out the noise.

Listening can be difficult. External noise and internal blockages can keep us from listening effectively. Some of us are afraid of investing the time and energy needed to listen deeply. Fear can keep us at a superficial level.[7] At the first sign of difficulty, we waver in our spiritual commitment.

A further impediment to really listening is clinging to past hurts, either real or imagined. The advantage to repeating the same pattern is that it is familiar. The threat of change is that we may have to confront our bitterness and angers and move into an unknown future.

A related obstacle to listening is our own self-centeredness. We can become preoccupied with our own needs and our own growth. True responsiveness to God leads to a certain self-forgetfulness as we listen to others. In so doing, we begin to relinquish control of our lives as we hand them over to God. Ultimately we realize that our own knowledge, training and insight, though very valuable, pale in comparison to God's call. God leads us most effectively.

To hear the call to spiritual growth, we need to slow down. The rush and noise of daily traffic can be deafening. Our inner and outer restlessness may prevent us from hearing God's call. We can find it difficult to sit still for ten minutes without a distracting telephone call or thought. In the constant busyness of our lives, it may not be easy to take the time to sit still and to listen.

Silence is cultivated in every religious tradition, and certainly in Christianity. It can help to remove us from our egotism and our preoccupations and enable us to seek God. Our restless desires and our greed—for information, knowledge or culture—are put into perspective in silence and prayerful reflection. Meditation and prayer can lead us more into God's time, which can be quite different from our own.

A member of the Vatican diplomatic corps once shared with me that he was very happy while assigned to a country in West Africa. He particularly loved going out of the capital to the priests' retreats in the countryside. If any of the priests were delayed, he recalled, the group would wait a day for them to arrive before starting the retreat. In contrast, his next assignment was in Germany where such meetings didn't start even a minute late. We might wonder what time schedule God follows.

Our impatience is often countered by God's deliberateness. A measure of our inner peace can be the extent to which we can begin to see that God's time is to be preferred.[8]

Spiritual Growth Calls for Patience[9]

A significant virtue of the spiritual life is patience. We are called to be patient with everyone, but first of all with ourselves. Spiritual growth takes time. Diligent effort, made without too much straining, offers the best hope of progress. Impetuous efforts, excessively energetic and frenetic, tend to spoil the very things we are trying to accomplish. Afterward, exhausted, we want to give up.

It seems better to begin each day anew rather than dwell on past faults and failings. Consistent application achieves results. Day to day, we vary in emotional energy, mood and physical strength (e.g., a little lack of sleep can really affect us). We need to do what we can on any given day to love God and serve our neighbor. As part of our morning planning for the day, we might look for ways to make the lives of those around us a bit easier or happier.

Our interest is in long-term formation of character, not incidental gain. St. Francis de Sales puts it well when he says:

> Just as a shrub that is often transplanted cannot take root and as a result cannot come to maturity and yield the desired fruit, so the soul that transplants its heart from plan to plan cannot profit or gain proper growth in perfection, since perfection does not consist in beginnings but in accomplishments.[10]

It seems best to choose a few areas of our lives and work on them persistently rather than dissipate our energies in a thousand different directions. As management consultants advise us, we need to "keep first things first."[11] If we need to spend more time with our children or visiting a sick relative, then we need to make that the first priority and put some projects at work or around the house on the back burner.

Each day we are called to faithfulness. This is especially true in regard to our particular vocation in life. Francis de Sales notes that

> ...every state of life is in some way irksome, bitter and unpleasant; and what is more, except for those who are wholly resigned to God's will, people are all inclined to want to change places with others.[12]

The task is to take the wearying duties of the present day (for me, this is dealing with the office mail) and turn them to our spiritual benefit; it is to live in the present moment and not in the nostalgic (or tragic) past or the imagined future; and it is to make the most of present relationships, challenges and opportunities.

Each day presents us with many occasions to practice small acts of kindness—to store clerks, ticket agents and other people we deal with—or of mercy or generous listening to those in need, distressed or upset. These little acts form and reform our character. They are the very texture of our daily lives and prepare us to face the major transitions of life.

Most spiritual growth is not spectacular and takes a long time. Our conversion rarely happens all at once as it did with St. Paul. For most people, it involves a lifetime of work with slow, solid and steady movement, not without occasional discouragements, which are to be expected. However, it is precisely how we deal with these setbacks that determines whether they will become opportunities or pitfalls.

Where does all this daily effort lead? It leads us closer to God and to a greater peacefulness and contentment. We become happier and we become easier to be around.

Growth with Others

This inner peace is very much manifest in how we relate to others. It shows itself in how we treat the people we meet each day and in our openness to learn from them. This begins early in life. I will always remember my brother-in-law telling me how he was surprised one day when he looked behind him and saw my little niece imitating the way he walked. He wasn't sure if this was good for her or not.

We learn by imitation. We see this in adults as well as in children. People imitate Elvis Presley, Michael Jordan or other superstars as well as fellow workers, family members and friends. Current controversies over the lyrics of music reflect the fact that we learn, for good or ill, from the example of those around us. If lyrics sung by popular stars degrade women, then they very well might lead their listeners to act in exploitative or disrespectful ways toward the women they meet.

The church proposes that people imitate saints because they embody the virtues that mark the Christian life. These individuals show us, quite practically, how to imitate Jesus. Good examples can be just as potent as bad.

Communities educate people for virtue or for vice. The community of drug dealers, for example, forms its members to an amoral standard by modeling and teaching the latest techniques for distributing drugs and evading the law. Young people so influenced are formed for violence.

Similarly, virtuous communities provide the interactions that instill positive ways—by the example of parents, neighbors and friends. Formal instruction can also play a major part by calling on people to do their best rather than condoning the not-so-good as acceptable. In education, the emphasis is on the truism that deeds make the man or woman. Choices determine the person. We must take responsibility for our lives.

In practice, our communities can be a mixture of virtue and vice. The conflicting models and messages we see around us can make growth in virtue a challenge. Part of our ongoing task is to work to make our communities more positive environments as we seek to grow spiritually ourselves.

As human persons we are made to be with others and, in fact, cannot come to happiness without a community. "The common good is that condition of peace, order, and economic sufficiency which provides happiness for all to the degree to which they can participate in it."[13] Our spiritual lives are very much formed in our interactions with individuals in our civic, work and religious communities.

Reason and Passion

One very important area of our communal formation is that of our emotions. Years ago a priest, now retired, shared an insight with me that I have come to believe is profoundly true. He said that people make most of their decisions based on how they feel, not on what they think. Our emotional lives are extremely important—perhaps more so than we would like to admit.

Virtue embraces both our emotions, classically referred to as our passions, and our reason.

...learning virtues is not just learning how to act....It is learning how to be moved (angered, shamed, delighted, drawn) by the right persons and things, to the right extent, for the right reasons, in the right way, at the right times.[14]

To speak of virtue is to speak of the integration, the proper balance, of reason and emotions—not of the control of one by the other. To speak of spiritual growth is to speak, paradoxically, of the importance of both our mind and our body. Rationality and bodiliness go together. In the virtuous life, our emotions are made more constant and our rationality is energized.

Such integration begins early in life.

Passions...are learned from early embodied interactions between infants and caregivers. The organism's dossier is first assembled in those interactions. And those learned, embodied passions then continue to *dispose* the organism to take its subsequent interactions with the other in a certain way.[15]

Our feelings are by their very nature interactive. Unless deliberately changed, our dispositions to interact with others and to feel in certain ways tend to stay with us. Perhaps this is why people who were abused as children, and have not experienced healing, have a tendency to repeat this behavior in adulthood. The patterns of interaction learned early in life tend to remain with us unless altered.

As we come to spiritual maturity, we may sense that our responses to other people are inappropriate or worse. At this point, we may choose to learn, in interactions with others, more effective ways of behaving. This relearning is not merely an intellectual rethinking and is not done all by ourselves. Rather, it involves our whole being. Support groups often seem to be the context for this relearning. Here we can see the importance of good spiritual friends in our religious communities or small groups with whom we can learn to act more appropriately and love more fully.

Ultimately, the mature person must see and approve his or her own actions, must take moral responsibility. Virtues such as patience and generosity can be learned by example in childhood but must be affirmed in adulthood and given an adult interpretation. Emotions and thoughts can be more thoroughly integrated in the virtuous life as we grow in relationships with others in our communities. We grow (or decline) throughout life in our practice of virtue. This growth is really growth in love. It is rooted in an appropriate love for self, matures in love for others, and reaches fulfillment in love for God. Such love, if it is true, manifests itself in deeds.

A couple I know has chosen to adopt a multihandicapped child no one wanted, and who has a short life expectancy. Such generous love is extraordinary to be sure. It involves infinite patience and confronts suffering— watching the child suffer and coming to grips with their own impotence. Yet the couple's love is a tremendous affirmation of life and speaks of a love that goes beyond personal pleasure to embrace a deeper meaning. We are here to go out of ourselves in love.

Imitating Christ

Essentially, in growing spiritually, in going out of ourselves in love, we become like Christ. Jesus is the model for our living and acting. We put our faith in him and his message of salvation. His love is the touchstone for our own; he is the point of reference. Our friendship with him is central to growing spiritually.

In seeking to be like Christ, we bring our talents and gifts. Each person has a different character, temperament, spiritual quality and history. Spiritual growth will be different for each of us, and we should not expect to be exactly the same as anyone else. We are not in competition with one another to be the only number one. Rather, we are in relationships where we are all called to finish the race and win the prize.

The race is arduous to be sure. Following Jesus leads to peace of heart and helps us to be peacemakers in a violent world. However, Jesus also leads us to the cross. We are called to make our action like his even to the point of dying, letting go of that which is most dear and loving completely—even to loving our enemies. This is the work of a lifetime.

Recently a friend shared with me his experience at a funeral home where the man being waked was in the same room where my friend's deceased wife had been viewed years earlier. This coincidence brought back to him a host of painful memories of those years where suffering and death were his close companions. He had had to let go of the person most dear to him. His path to deeper spiritual maturity had covered some very difficult terrain.

The path to such spiritual maturity, to growth in virtue, is the way of relationships. Our friendships with Christ, with spouse, with others and with self give the dynamism to our spiritual lives. Our growth in faith is not apart from the world but in the midst of it. Our growth in virtue is not apart from pain but in its midst. Our inner peace grows not apart from others but in the midst of them.

QUESTIONS FOR REFLECTION AND DISCUSSION

1. How well do you listen? What are your predominant obstacles to listening?

2. How do you feel most days? Is there one feeling that is most prominent in your life? Where does this feeling originate?

3. Could you name an experience of suffering that has led you to spiritual growth?

III. Friendship with Self

Good friendships in solid communities are absolutely necessary for us to come to spiritual maturity. The major theme of this book is that our formation comes in relationships. Our deepest questions about our lives are not answered in isolation but in interaction. Friendship at its best impels us forward on the spiritual journey. Friends challenge us to spiritual growth.

We begin our discussion with ourselves as individuals. This is how we see ourselves. In the course of these chapters, we will explore our friendships and acknowledge that there is much to recommend describing ourselves in terms of our relationships as well as in a résumé of our accomplishments and education. We are both our individuality and our relatedness.

The topic of friendship with self is sometimes neglected in works that deal explicitly with friendship.[1] Yet in our culture we begin with ourselves. And there is ample justification for this in Christian history. Great saints such as Augustine often looked deeply within themselves for God's grace so that they might be better able to go out to others. The two movements are not mutually exclusive but complementary. Made in God's image, we can always become more appreciative of the gifts we have and the graces we have received. True humility acknowledges our blessings. We are flawed to be sure but also redeemed. In appreciating our inner strength, our giftedness, and God's grace, we gain strength for reaching out to others.

The danger for us in our therapeutic culture is that we will remain stuck on analyzing or improving ourselves. There is a danger that we will become self-absorbed or narcissistic, never getting beyond ourselves. In an environment so influenced by advertising that stresses pleasure, we might find it easy just to stay focused on ourselves and our wants. We can become quite acquisitive; we need the latest in everything. We might begin to think that fast cars, fashionable clothes, or the latest software will make us happy. Just as with smoking, we eventually discover that making possessions primary in our lives can have lethal long-term effects. Hopefully, the experience of the loneliness and emptiness of the acquisitive self can begin to bring us to our senses. We begin to realize that possessions and pleasures have their place but are not the primary one in life.

If we are aware of the pitfalls of looking at ourselves, we also are aware of the benefits and necessity of doing so. If we are to grow in relationships with God and others, we must come to know ourselves. In fact, our self-knowledge is not separate from our other relationships. As we gain insight into ourselves and our gifts, we are more readily able to share them with others. In coming to know others and God, we come to know ourselves better. As we will see, our relationship with self, others and God are intertwined, not separate.

Coming to Know Ourselves

…the transformation from self-concern into true self-love is always a thing of the Spirit. It is a breaking open of the shell of ourselves that means rebirth and a radical reorientation in love.[2]

Our reorientation is an ongoing process and involves many dimensions. In it, we both collaborate with the grace of the Holy Spirit and work to utilize our gifts.

One dimension in befriending ourselves is getting to know our own patterns of thinking and acting. As we grow older, these may come more into focus. We become more aware of our emotional reactions and seek out their roots. We notice our preoccupations and wonder why this set of concerns is so important to us. We begin to realize and admit that the faults we see in others are often in ourselves.

When I return home to visit my parents, I notice how much I am like them. I have picked up many of my patterns from them. I speak on the telephone just as my father did when I was growing up. A friend whose parent was an alcoholic noticed later in life that his emotional reaction—particularly in moments of stress—was to try to please everyone just as he had tried to do in growing up in an unstable home environment.

Whatever the origin of our patterns of thinking and acting, once we become aware of them, we can make some choices. I'm happy to speak like my father on the telephone. My friend prefers to develop new ways of relating to others in stressful situations that are more appropriate to what is actually going on.

In making these choices, we have to avoid the human tendency to blame the negative on someone else. Our parents, the boss, our spouse or anybody may have affected how we act, but what we do now is our responsibility. We can choose, with the help of others, to begin to think and act differently. In addition, in coming to self-awareness, we may also come to a certain realism about what we can and cannot do. We may choose to live within our limitations. Our ways of dealing with things may not be optimal but they may be sufficient. Which changes in our lives are worth the effort? This is the question of priorities. How shall I expend my limited energies, especially as I get older?

In regard to all this self-examination, it is important not to lose our sense of humor. The foolish or even "crazy" person in my environs is occasionally me! "To be able to understand how adolescent most of us are at least some of the time is the human faculty that finally makes us lovable."[3] Perfection is for heaven and many times we just have to shake our heads at our own imperfections. How many of us have shown up to do a good work on the wrong day? Once I took a two-hour train ride to attend a meeting that had occurred the day before!

Our sense of irony is also honed as we look at our lives. Some of us who thought we were moving away from a certain style of life have seen ourselves embrace it under a new guise. For instance, priests and religious sisters and brothers who have taken a vow of poverty precisely to escape the pressures of money and finances often find themselves devoting large amounts of their time to raising funds for a parish, hospital, school or other good work. God's ways are not our ways and God's sense of humor is sometimes in evidence. A little humor can give us perspective on the unexpected but far from disastrous aspects of our lives.

Time for Knowing Oneself

If we are to attain the balance and humor of true self-love, we need to take some time for self-examination. Finding this time outside retirement can be quite difficult in contemporary America. We are busy and tend to ignore our need for solitude to reflect, to pray and to examine our lives.

Sometimes we must ask ourselves whether all our *busyness* makes a difference.[4] Or is it destructive of self and others? Are we prisoners of the exhilaration of being busy and rushing from place to place? We love the sense of energy and excitement our lifestyle brings. All the while we have the illusion of being firmly in control of our lives. Yet in the rush, we often fail to notice the things and people around us. We walk right by them. And in our more reflective moments we wonder if we may be failing at the most important things while managing our time to make the less important things turn out all right. Are we dodging the personal questions and the relationships that give life meaning by immersing ourselves in lists of things to do?

The alternative I would propose would be more attentive seeing and listening. We could take time to listen to our interior feelings and needs. We could pay more attention to the world that surrounds us and startles us with its beauty. We could stop to really listen to others rather than giving a perfunctory nod while all the while thinking of our next event or project. We could reach out more to others in kind words and gentle deeds.

A central question today is whether a relaxed and prayerful attitude is not more beneficial for us in the long run. Paying attention to all of reality can be enriching for self and others. Might we not need to make some choices that point us in this direction? Might having more information or more accessibility through technology *not* be the way to go? Sometimes we might do well to leave the portable phone at the office. And maybe we should occasionally skip the next meeting, turn the computer off and have lunch with an old friend.

Our busyness shows an inner restlessness. We are not

quite at ease with ourselves and the world. There must be something more. *When these questions begin to arise, we are ripe for spiritual renewal.* Yet, a true spiritual life brings both happiness and cost. It calls us to be honest with ourselves, to let go of accustomed ways of thinking and acting, and to make commitments to change. A generosity is required for the spiritual and moral life that runs counter to a pure ethic of pragmatism and pleasure.

Change can be both exhilarating and difficult. The effect of previous character formation and the presence or absence of moral principles both in us and around us can have a tremendous impact on our daily lives. Most of us still struggle to unlearn patterns of acting acquired when we were young.

Societies obviously can have similar problems as they struggle with the long-term effects of an ideology such as Nazism or Communism on social attitudes and behaviors. While on a trip to Romania for example, I learned that if you lived there during the Ceausescu regime, you had to be careful to conceal the truth. Even today people can still be wary with strangers although the situation has changed. Deeply ingrained patterns often take a long time to alter.

We continuously renew our spiritual quest, knowing that we are called to change. We believe that our spiritual journey will answer our deepest questions. To accomplish needed changes, it is important to take some time for our spiritual selves. This may be as much as a weekend retreat or as little as a few minutes a day for spiritual reflection. The time available varies by vocation but also by temperament. A half-hour of quiet, reflective time would seem to be necessary to settle down and then to pray. But we do what we can with the time available. We need some time at least occasionally for a relaxed examination of our inner selves.

In today's world, it can be difficult to find such rest.[5] We always have one more letter to write or phone call to make. We have to do things ourselves and have trouble delegating tasks and projects to others even when they might do a better job. We tell ourselves that we must have everything completed in order to relax. And rarely can we get everything in order.

Certainly much hard work is called for as we seek to live Christ's message in our world. The Christian is no stranger to hard work and long days. Such purposeful activity is necessary and fulfills our deepest longings as human beings. We are never so happy as when pursuing a strongly motivating goal. As beings in God's image, we are made to go out of ourselves to others and to build a community.

What is necessary is balance. There is a proper rhythm to work and rest. Excessive rest may imply self-centeredness and self-indulgence. Excessive work may imply that our trust is in self and not in God. Rest has to do with feeling safe, with trusting. We learn trust or distrust from an early age. As we grow to adulthood, we are called more and more to put our trust in God—no easy task. Learning to trust in God's love is ongoing. I'm continually forgetting God's presence and love and lapsing into the activism of doing it all myself.

To be effectively active, we must take time to listen to our interior selves, to the words of others and to God. We need to spend time in prayer in its various forms.

Letting Go

A critical issue in coming to peace of heart and to spiritual growth is learning to let go.[6] This is the lesson of a lifetime. We begin to learn to let go in our infancy. My youngest niece has learned to walk. To do so, she had to let go of the sofa and take a step. She learned something new—and not without a few falls.

This pattern repeats itself throughout life. There is the challenge and our response, which can occur when our successor at work or in our volunteer activities appears on the scene. We feel like the prophet Elijah might have when God picked his successor Elisha (1 Kgs 19:19–21). The appearance of our successor can tell us that this phase of our life is at an end. Unlike Elijah, we will probably not complete our tenure by going to heaven in a fiery chariot. Our endings are much more mundane. It can be difficult to accept that a phase or period or project is coming to an end but it also might be an opportunity for something new.

The same is true in our interior lives. We can go deeper if we can let go of the past, which can be extremely difficult to do in practice. As we see the patterns and attitudes in our lives that call for change, we need to release them. But even if we clearly see the need for change, it can be difficult. The same old rut may not be comfortable but it is familiar.

We often need to turn to God for help in this process and to our friends as well. Here the time we have set aside for meditation can be crucial.

> By coming to a deeper awareness of what God is calling us to we can learn to let go of what is blocking us. Such awareness comes primarily in prayer, where God reveals Himself to us. The power of His love becomes an irresistible force which draws us out of ourselves and into God. Concern for self lessens as we become more filled with the divine presence.[7]

A critical point for this process is embracing the new. Every challenge to let go presents an opportunity to replace the old with the new. Failed ways of acting can give way to the successful. Old projects can yield to the new just as old skepticisms can give way to new commitments. Recently a friend accepted an offer of early retirement from a job he had grown to despise. Now he is very gratified as he volunteers time to work with the dying at a local hospice.

Befriending ourselves involves "becoming." We gradually become a renewed person. The process of change, of letting go and taking up, is a continuing one. We learn the limits of the self and the gifts we have to share. We also are consciously stretching ourselves. In part we are accepting the suffering and loss that come from change. A businessman put it very well to me one night when he said that in his life he was now "walking toward the cross." Previously he had run away; he avoided his ethical responsibilities at work. Now he found walking right toward the cross more effective. He was accepting the challenges Jesus offered him.

Our walk does not have to be alone because friends walk with us and help us through the suffering and the joy that accompany change. In fact, our friends can be those who can most help us achieve authentic friendship with the self. So it is to human friendship that we now turn.

QUESTIONS FOR REFLECTION AND DISCUSSION

1. What are some of the patterns in your life? Where did they come from? Do some of them need to be changed?

2. What patterns in your life might you need to hang on to?

3. Can you carve out some time each day or week for personal prayer and reflection?

IV. Friendship with Others

*I*f we take a minute or two, we can name those people who have been most influential in our lives. Among this number will be our best friends, the people who have influenced us the most, especially in adulthood.

I remember meeting Al and Cathy for the first time on the front step of the local parish where I was helping one Sunday morning. They were friends of the associate pastor, who is a good friend of mine. He introduced us. She suggested that I come for dinner—usually a well-intended but meaningless pleasantry. Much to my surprise, she gave me their phone number. From these incidental beginnings began a friendship that lasted for many years until Cathy died, and which still continues with Al to this day.

Though it is a common experience, friendship is not easy to define. Perhaps this is because they vary in type and development. Friendships profoundly influence our spiritual growth. We will discuss a few types as we proceed and devote a later chapter to spiritual friendship.

Friendships cannot be planned and most often happen spontaneously as they did for me with Al and Cathy. I have known a few people who, realizing the need for friends in their lives, have deliberately tried to make them. In general, these relationships have failed. I don't know exactly why. However, it is true that there is a certain spontaneity to friendship that cannot be overly programmed.

I also believe that because of our individual talents and

gifts, we are capable of friendship with certain people and not with others. This is not so much a function of time available but of differences of personality or of needs. While being kind and generous with all, we need not and cannot be friends with everyone.

On getting to know a few individuals, I have found that they remain acquaintances rather than friends. In some, there was such an inordinate need for time and attention due to past (negative) life experiences that no individual could meet that need in friendship. For others, the need to dominate or control relationships was so strong that a sensitive and supportive mutual communication was impossible. Of course, these tendencies are not immediately apparent as we encounter others. Time usually brings such personal patterns to our awareness.

Some people are almost friendless though you might never know it from a chance encounter. They have never learned how to be friends in a meaningful way. Others have outlived their friends or moved to another part of the country away from such ties. These people are often quite vulnerable to arguments from social utility or so-called "quality of life" that cause them to question their worth and make them wonder if it might not be better to "end it all," especially if they are elderly and faced with pain or suffering. Loneliness can be devastating for any of us and can enhance our dark feelings of despair. Relationships are necessary for our well being, and even a superficial acquaintanceship may make quite a difference for a lonely person.

Some General Characteristics of Friendship

Good friendships tend to bring out the best in us and can be the engines for our spiritual growth. Meeting Al and Cathy had a long-term and most positive effect on my spiritual life. They introduced me to a circle of friends and to the Cursillo movement, a type of spiritual renewal with which I was unacquainted. This certainly was not the only influence in my life but it was a central one.

Friendships affect us by their *communication,* both verbal and nonverbal. As we do with them, friends share with us their ideas, interests, projects and concerns. These may be of monumental importance or of the day-to-day variety. Such sharings presume a significant level of trust.

We respond to friends by *listening attentively.* Just as we need to listen to ourselves (to our own thoughts, feelings and patterns), we need to listen to friends. This is listening with head and heart and includes a receptivity to personal differences. It requires a commitment to our friends and their well-being because we know that it can be difficult to listen—especially when we are tired or discouraged. A friend may call just as we are ready to retire for the evening, and it can require a great effort of will to pay even half-attention.

We respond to friends by *respecting their separateness.* At times our friends need some solitude, time to be alone. We can facilitate and encourage this aspect of our relatedness, knowing that it can be of great help to them in befriending themselves and coming to inner maturity.

Friends encourage us to be our best selves. They not only support us in new ventures or in difficulties but also challenge us to examine our patterns or our potentialities. Friends elaborate, modify or even question our ideas and plans. They force us to think them through again. Many a disaster is avoided this way. I've had a couple of acquaintances who, against the advice of friends, have gone into business for themselves and failed. Likewise, I've seen others who, with friends' encouragement, have developed their own businesses and succeeded. There are no guarantees of course, but the advice of friends, those who have our well-being at heart, is worth major consideration in times of transition or of new initiatives in our lives.

Friends can often recognize our patterns and characteristic ways of acting better than we can ourselves. They can help us to see ourselves more clearly. At times, they will challenge us to leave behind our self-destructive ways. For example, they sometimes intervene in a friend's slide into depression or alcoholism and guide the person to needed therapy. Such challenges can be risky for a friendship. Perhaps the relationship will be altered significantly or destroyed if we interfere in difficult areas in a friend's life. Some things we just don't want to hear; neither do our friends.

At other times, friends will encourage us to use our talents more fully or to develop others. For example, they often encourage one another to go back to school to hone a skill. They can offer needed cheers and support when we are unsure of our ability in a new arena and are doubting ourselves.

Friends know one another's flaws and accept them. While sometimes challenging, they are also accepting up to a point. Friends don't want to absorb our flaws; they have enough of their own. They accept who we are and give us time to work to become our best selves. Friends show us compassion; they feel for us in our difficulties.

Relationships can change dramatically or subtly. The unexpected discovery of a disease such as cancer can alter the focus of a friendship. What changes one person—alters ways of thinking, causes preoccupation or precipitates the drafting of a will—inexorably affects the other in the relationship. Feelings of disengagement to avoid hurt or of impotence in the face of suffering or of anger with God may intrude into the friendship.

"To live is to change" the saying goes. Major events,

either positive or negative, call for adjustments that are ulti-mately enriching but momentarily exhausting. Friendships do not stay the same. We grow or decline in our relation-ships over time.

Friendships are most important in our lives, yet to be fruitful must go beyond themselves. They need to embrace a larger cause, to serve the good and to make an institution better. Adam and Eve were to be cocreators with God, stewards of the earth, until they decided for self-interest and self-indulgence. Immediately their relationship fell apart and they started blaming each other.

Spiritual Growth through Friendship

Friendship is a form of love, in which we become like the ones we love. I enjoy kidding engaged couples that eventu-ally they will come to "look like each other" if they love long enough. It is true that in the mutuality of friendship we do begin to share in one another's qualities and resem-ble each other inside.

Such inner resemblance may be for ill or good. If we communicate "false goods,"[1] then we may become vicious rather than holy. For example, this is the sharing of the drug gang or, perhaps more to the point, those who use drugs together at parties and social gatherings, promoting both the drug cartels and mutual dissolution.

Some relationships can be more frivolous than anything else. They are superficial and waste time. Of course, wast-ing a little time can be the generous or charitable thing to do. But we do this with the realization that while diver-sions are necessary, friendships are substantive.

The Catholic tradition argues that while we are to be char-itable to all, we should "befriend only those with whom [we] can be mutually supportive in virtue."[2] Friendship is at the core of our growth in virtue—our spiritual and moral growth—and we should be careful whom we choose to befriend because we will become like them. We will share various levels of friendship throughout our lives and among these we will need the spiritual friendships that help to make us holy. They are

> ...spiritual friendships by which two or more persons mutually communicate their supernatural affection and their love of God, and have only one heart and only one soul.[3]

Such relationships tend to be simple and direct. These friends are quite open and readily share their gifts with others. They are recognizable in their imitation of Christ and help one another to become more and more like him.

We are called to bring all our friendships into Christ in an appropriate way. This gradually calls for an end to possessiveness, which we may find quite difficult to attain in practice, and concomitantly an opening out to share our love and talents more broadly. Love always reaches out generously to others and true love encourages friends to reach out as well.

Friendship with Colleagues

Friendships are of many types and dimensions. It is impossible to summarize them all. Yet we can reflect on certain familiar types as we seek insight into our own friendships.

Most of us have experienced the *friendship for a time*. We meet someone, often a colleague or a collaborator in some project, with whom we have a splendid relationship, but whose presence in our life is only temporary. I have found this in certain church renewal movements, such as the

Cursillo. A team comes together, works assiduously for a few months to build a small community, shares its faith with others on a retreat weekend and then returns to normal ways of living. The people have common goals and high ideals and share their lives with one another but most often only for a time. Such short-term friendships are life-forming and exhilarating. They influence us for the good but do not generally persist.

Other types of *colleagueship* are more long-lasting. We work together with other individuals and share some common interests and concerns.

> Often it is a way of *being,* of being with another, a sense that someone asks the same questions as you do, with the same intent, and that you will find both a stimulation of interest in whatever you are looking at together, as well as a comfort and richness of appreciation that satisfies an old longing for home.[4]

The friendship of colleagues drives us forward to grow both professionally and personally. The colleague is the person with whom we can have a detailed discussion of the issues in our field of endeavor whether that be engineering or cultural history or youth ministry. A colleague is one who can share with us his or her expertise and lead us into new understandings or appreciation of our areas of interest or concern. Occasionally, a group of colleagues can have one of those spontaneous discussions that leaves each person with new insights into the connections between our varied areas of competency.

We often limit friendships with colleagues to the work environment. The relationships have a certain definition unlike that of marriage and family, which are much more all-embracing. Colleagueship, sometimes referred to as collaboration in church circles, is a more specific and defined relationship than marriage.

Since our human work helps make us who we are, sharing it with colleagues and collaborators can be quite important. The work shapes us as we do the work. "...toil is sometimes a drudgery, and even sometimes dangerous, it is still good for people to engage in. Why? Because, through our work we become a partner with God in bringing creation to perfection."[5] In working together we also work with God. The unity of friendship with self, others and God can be evident in our labor. The world of work, or at least our little part of it, can be oriented to the good by virtuous colleagues.

Marital Friendships

The most significant relationship of men and women in our culture is marriage—even though it has been under fire for quite some time now in favor of "freer" forms of love. Most people still desire marriage. "...the idea of a marriage of opposites, of man and woman in soul and body, expresses our deepest hopes for wholeness and unity in this life."[6] This type of union goes beyond rational explanations and expresses the deepest mystery of the person.

Good marriages tend to show those qualities of deep friendship mentioned above. They have a profound quality of communication. One of the "languages" that expresses this is sexuality, which also embodies commitment to one another and to the next generation. At its best, the sexual union reflects the deep friendship of the couple.

Such friendships, as all others, have many practical details to be worked out again and again on the journey through life. Each person is separate but together they are a unity. Each comes with a different background and needs.

Many women have a circle of friends with whom they speak regularly. Men tend not to have best friends;[7] they focus on achieving results with colleagues and rely on their wives for close friendship and support.

Couples have a need for both time together and time alone, which becomes difficult in our contemporary busy work environment. Sometimes couples who work outside the home go for days with little contact because of differing schedules. Add to this the demands of children and time for each other can be at a minimum or even nonexistent. Times for prayer together or for sharing beyond the daily details of life can be very few. On the other hand, some retired couples are together all the time and must be attentive to each other's need for some time apart.

One key in marriage and in many other types of relationships seems to be balance. We need to figure out our priorities and work things out in an ongoing way. Communication with the spouse, not presuming that he or she can read our minds, is essential. This is especially true for the little things that go so much into making our relationships with one another work. Marriage provides ample opportunities for practicing the virtues of patience, gentleness, generosity and self-sacrifice. "Above all, the family embodies a repudiation of individualism since it can only function along principles of altruism, self-sacrifice, deferred gratification and selfless love."[8] True marital union stands contrary to the underlying values driving much of modern culture.

Friendships of Men and Women

Similar principles of altruism and generosity make possible nonmarital friendships between men and women as embodied in those of the saints such as Clare and Francis of Assisi, Francis de Sales and Jane de Chantal.

Some today, as in ancient times, would question the possibility of friendship between men and women outside marriage. One modern author contends that "economic, political, psychological, and other differences between the genders result in the fact that women find it difficult to be friends with men and vice versa."[9]

Many others contend that such friendships are possible though men and women must be aware of the pitfalls. Most generally discussed is the role of Eros. Erotic attachment tends to move the friends toward marriage or to destroy their relationship. Eros implies exclusivity while true friendship is open to others. This is not to say that there is not a certain excitement in good man-woman relationships absent from other forms of friendship.

Besides excitement, differing perceptions and priorities may also exist between men and women, which can be quite enriching but also exasperating. One recent author suggests that "for men life is 'a struggle to preserve independence,' while for women it is a struggle to preserve intimacy.'"[10] Further, in times of difficulty, women may want to share their perceptions and feelings, while men see a problem that needs to be solved. These are generalizations that do not apply to every individual, but differences do exist between people.

> Our world is full of attempts, not always terribly humorous, to remove such differences from life. In [Deborah] Tannen's words, "Sensitivity training judges men by women's standards and tries to get them to talk more like women. Assertiveness training judges women by men's standards and tries to get them to talk more like men." Better, perhaps, she suggests, to learn to understand and accept each other.[11]

Such a suggestion is quite important in an age when more and more men and women work together in the market-place. Men and women at their best can learn from each other in colleagueship and deeper types of friendship.

> Each…needs a certain maturity: a sense of who they are, what they really want, what is the nature of their freely chosen vocation, and to whom their primary commitment is given. Beyond this, they need a heightened sense of each other's lived contexts: who else does my friend love, what is the total range of his or her concerns, the demands on time and energy to which he or she must respond to be fully him or herself?[12]

Friendships between men and women can prosper when rooted in God and focused on developing spiritually together in a wider community, when they are not exclusive but inclusive, open to the input and concerns of others. Friendships succeed when external projects help people to focus on wider communal and civic concerns, and give them much to talk over and focus on. Friendships can prosper when they are willing to "let go" in accepting that suffering and self-denial are part of their relationship as with every other.

Friendships between men and women give us great insight into the other's way of thinking and acting. In taking us out of ourselves, they can help us to be more balanced and sane than we might otherwise be.

Collaboration in Ministry

An emerging area of friendship and colleagueship is that of collaboration in ministry. Increasingly men and women, clerics, religious and laity are working together for the good of the parish, hospital, school or other community.

Relationships in this context are often, but not always, quite fruitful. Differences of personality, style and gifts can lead to strife and even dissolution of the parish team just as in any other work environment.

More positively, the situation offers challenges and opportunities. Men and women working together can have strengths in perception and action that neither has individually. The dialogue in mutuality between colleagues can impel spiritual growth. Ministry done in a collaborative context can have greater balance and dynamism.

Catholicism is still challenged by this context. Some priests, for example, struggle with the issue of women's role in the church because they've been educated and trained in a largely woman-free environment. Lay people, some remembering the not-so-distant days of "pray, pay and obey" may be reluctant to exercise leadership. Women, too, sometimes struggle with questions of their real leadership role in an era that has seen greater participation by them at all levels in society.

Opportunities abound that offer a truly collaborative leadership of service. The recent papal "apology" for historical negligence and sin[13] toward women, and the American bishops' invitation to theologians to explore new ways women can participate in church leadership,[14] are creating an opening for mutual growth and greater balance and equanimity. The traditional extremes of patriarchy are now equaled by some feminist extremes that abandon the central elements of Christianity.[15] A more fruitful context for discussion might be—not men and women in isolation—but men and women working together as colleagues or friends. For instance, if a bishop has no women in the inner circle of the diocese where decisions really are made or if a sister hospital president has no men in her inner circle, I would question whether the gifts and talents of the community are being properly used.

Collaboration in ministry is a complex and fascinating aspect of the current church and its growth. It is one contemporary dimension of our ongoing need to learn to be friends with one another. For the Christian, the context of this search for friendship and love is prayer. We turn now to our relationship with God in friendship and mutual communication.

QUESTIONS FOR REFLECTION AND DISCUSSION

1. A student of mine, a mature businessman, questions whether friendship is as important to spiritual growth as I make it out to be. Is there spiritual growth without friendship? What do you think?

2. What has been the role of friends in your own life?

3. What types of friendship have we missed in our discussion above?

4. To what sort of people do you find yourself drawn? What makes friendship with them an attraction? How have you found yourself different because of your friendships?

5. If you have been involved in collaborative ministry, what has been your experience of the colleagueship involved?

V. Friendship with God

*Y*ears ago, when I was a young seminarian doing part-time pastoral work, I went to a parish lecture. The speaker, a woman from the parish, was addressing a group of teenagers and their parents about God. The gist of her talk was that "our God is too small." What I took away from that presentation was the realization that we are always in need of expanding our conception of God. The God of the universe is beyond our complete comprehension and can always be understood more fully.

More recently, a writer wrote of the "God of her understanding."[1] I believe that this way of speaking is both realistic and deficient. Yes, we do have our own conception of God based on our learning and experience. God is known to us, but God who is mystery is so much more than our limited conceptions. Our understanding of the revelation about God, especially through Jesus, broadens our conception of who God is and challenges our tendency to subjectivism, to making God in our image and likeness, deflecting those demands that we find too uncomfortable.

Now that I am older, what I also understand better is that our knowledge of God embraces our whole being. God through his son Jesus wants to enter into friendship with us. He wants a more complete personal relationship with us, especially in prayer. In the Holy Spirit, we are responding or trying to respond to this invitation to friendship.

God's Presence

To speak of friendship with God is to speak of friendship in a somewhat different sense than in our previous chapters but no less truly. Jesus tells us, as he told Martha, Mary, Lazarus and the disciples, that we too are his friends (see Jn 15:13–15). "It is in and through Christ, his work on the cross, his love extended to us from the Father, that we are called to be friends with God."[2] Jesus provides us our window into God; he shows us the Father.

"The neutering approach depersonalizes God. It leaves us with a cold, distant shell of a God, totally alien to the God whom Jesus...called 'Abba'...."[3] How we think about God is too limited if we exclude the warmth of Jesus' relationship to his Father. It is best to start with the God of Jesus Christ and with Jesus himself. His life is our best window into God.

God is with us and speaks to us. This communication comes in a variety of ways. God speaks to us *through scripture.* God speaks to us *through tradition* as inspired by the Holy Spirit. God speaks to us *in the quiet (or the uproar) of our hearts.*

Scripture is God's inspired word for us. At times the biblical word almost leaps off the page to console or challenge us amidst the events of our daily lives. As we read and meditate on the vast riches of this holy word, especially in the New Testament, we hear God speak to us directly and insistently. Slowly, our very way of viewing reality is formed by daily encounters with the biblical word. I distinctly remember walking by a beggar who was asking for money at the subway station early one morning. I didn't give him any. Later, I wondered if I was "the priest who walked by" in the parable of the Good Samaritan. Our dialogue with God's word eventually forms our way of looking at things.

If God speaks to us directly through the inspired word, he also speaks to us through our *Spirit-guided tradition.* Down through history the work of the Holy Spirit has continued. The Spirit can and does speak definitively to our Christian community. For example, we know now very clearly that slavery is wrong.

The work of the Spirit, often expressed in ecumenical councils, is codified in documents and professions of faith, such as the Nicene Creed. The most recent, and imperfect as always, attempt to capture the Catholic tradition is in the *Catechism of the Catholic Church.* God can and does speak to us through such documents and they deserve our prayerful reflection.[4]

The poet Jessica Powers refers to God's presence *within us* as *this trackless solitude*

> Deep in the soul the acres lie
> of virgin lands, or sacred wood
> where waits the Spirit. Each soul bears
> this trackless solitude.[5]

God is always with us, in our deepest being, even when we feel most alone. In a way particular to each person, God speaks to us heart-to-heart.

God speaks to us *through nature* both physical and human. The well-known Jesuit poet Gerard Manley Hopkins "looked hard at things until they looked back at him, revealing within the process the mysterious, glorious, sometimes terrible presence of the God who stood behind and within nature."[6] I have found that the beauty of a sunset or of the distant mountains speaks to me of the grandeur and magnificence of God. Reflecting on the immensity of the expanding universe makes me conscious of the relative insignificance of what I do, thereby causing humility and relieving anxiety within me.

Though God speaks to us in many ways, it is *through others* that we most often hear his voice—through the members of the various civil and religious communities of which we are a part. These may include those who oppose us or our closest colleagues and collaborators. A friend told me recently that the most creative person she knows is a deeply prayerful colleague who inspires her to take her concerns and ideas to prayer. God has spoken to her though the colleague is unaware that her example has conveyed this message.

Though in some ways different, our friendship with God also shares many common elements with the friendship with others mentioned in the previous chapter. There is communication, reciprocity and suffering in our friendships both with God and with others, a need for spending time with each other and for always learning more about our friend.

> What happens in any friendship is that in some ways the friends become more alike, in some ways they become increasingly different. As friendships grow, likeness increases inasmuch as the interests, concerns, values, and ideals of the friends become similar. On the other hand difference increases too, because the deeper and longer our friendships with others, the more we become ourselves. The same is true in our friendship with God. We become more like God because we come to love what God loves, we make God's good our own; but we also become more unlike God because we become more genuinely ourselves.[7]

Our friendship with God reflects who we are and who we wish to become. Basically, we are always the same person. We are consistent. The way we think about ourselves is most likely the way we think about God and others. The way we act toward others will likely be consistent with the way we act toward God. If our God is essentially a lawgiver, we most probably are concerned with how we and others keep the law. If we always arrive breathless and late for appointments, we most likely come to God with our concerns at the last possible minute. If we tend to be demanding of others, we most likely are demanding of ourselves and see God as demanding great things of us. In looking more deeply at our conception of God and our communication with him, we learn about ourselves as well.

Our Response to God

We respond to God's presence in many different ways. Our response depends on what God is saying to us and this is an individual conversation. Made for love, we reach out to others in a gentle and respectful way. Love is not selfish but self-giving. Our response to God may in fact be in recognizing that some deed is to be done. For example, our prayerful discernment of God's call might lead us to choose to work as the treasurer of a Catholic school. Or we might listen in church to a parable of Jesus healing the sick and know that we must visit an acquaintance in a nursing home. In our activity in life, we can and do respond to God's communication with daily acts of gentleness and kindness to our neighbor.

Our most characteristic response to God's communication is in prayer. Just as Jesus prayed and called his disciples to prayer, we are to pray. Prayer is familiar to most of us through such as the "Our Father," but we might find it difficult to define prayer precisely. It affects and changes us and seems, as a relationship with God, to move us out of ourselves to others. St. Francis de Sales spoke of prayer in this fashion:

I am not taking the word "prayer" in this context merely in the sense of "petition" or "the request for some benefit that the faithful express in God's presence," as St. Basil describes it. I mean what St. Bonaventure meant when he said that prayer, widely speaking, embraces the whole of contemplative activity; what St. Gregory of Nyssa meant when he taught that "prayer is an interview or conversation between the soul and God"; …and finally, what St. Augustine and St. [John] Damascene meant when they said that prayer is "an ascent, or uplifting of the mind toward God." If prayer is a talk or conversation between the soul and God, then in prayer we talk to God and God also speaks to us; we aspire to him and he inspires us; we are alive to him and he lives in us.[8]

Our Life of Prayer

Our life of prayer can and does take a variety of forms. How we pray flows from our personality and experience, though it seems likely that we pray in different ways depending on the occasion and circumstances.

Sometimes we say *prayers that we know by heart* such as the "Our Father." Similarly, Catholics pray the Rosary. The constant repetition of prayers known by rote frees the mind to reflect on the mysteries of salvation or on the individuals for whom we might be praying. My Aunt Margaret used to have a collection of prayer cards. She would pray these every day in memory of the deceased or for some special intention or good work that she thought should be kept in prayer.

My friend Ron has his "top ten" intentions that he writes down and tries to keep in mind each day. He reworks these from week to week as the situations change of those he remembers in prayer.

Other times we might pray more spontaneously from

the heart in thanksgiving for the blessings we have received. Or we might enter into *conversation with God.* At one time, I had a friend who was angry with God over the impending dissolution of her marriage. I asked her how she prayed. She said that she recited the psalms (a wonderful way of praying). I suggested that in her prayer she might mention to God her anger at the breakup of her marriage. After all, why would she think God didn't know how she felt? She did eventually do this and found it both freeing and consoling. In our conversational prayer, we pray as who we are and not as the person we think we ought to be. As in any relationship, honesty counts.

Many people pray individually by reflection on the scriptures. This may be through the classic method called *lectio divina* where one reads the scriptures until a certain passage stands out and calls for reflection. After reflecting for awhile, the person continues until the next passage strikes him or her, and so on. Such prayer is excellent for forming our mind in the scriptures and can be done in connection with a commentary, so that we might be seeking divine guidance through praying the scriptures as they can be best understood. I personally find this to be a helpful method of praying, as God's word frequently comes alive for me here.

Reflection on scripture might also take the form of one of the methods of *meditation.*[9] These often involve using our imagination to "see" a scriptural passage and to connect with the mystery and activity of Christ in the scene. This type of prayer is more affective than analytical. It best concludes with a good daily resolution that tries to put our spiritual goodwill into concrete action.

Beyond organized meditation, we have *contemplation.* Nowadays it is seen as not limited to the great saints but as more readily accessible to the spiritual person. One form of this is dwelling in the presence of God—just being there. It is a wordless presence to the great mystery of God's presence with us in Christ. St. Jane de Chantal practiced this form of prayer to profound effect. It reflects the just-being-there aspect of any profound friendship, where presence is important and words unnecessary.

Community Prayer

The personal prayer we have just briefly discussed leads to and nourishes community prayer. In turn, communal prayer leads to personal prayer. Both are our response to God and sustain us in our day-to-day activities in the world.

Prayer leads to action that leads to prayer. We pray about our experiences and for the people and situations we encounter. Our communal prayer sustains our personal prayer. Our life *is,* or more likely *seeks to be,* a prayer-filled unity, not a compartmentalized diversity or fragmentation. At our best, we approach our whole day and all its actions with a prayerful spiritual attitude.

People today often share their prayer in *small groups.* These may be for bible study or for the spiritual growth of couples or for praising God in prayer or the like. They may be relatively large or rather small. Such groups have a certain intimacy and level of trust as the members share their faith with one another. God can speak very strongly through these groups, which are such that they can encourage and support growth in virtue. They are a broadening of spiritual friendships to a community.

Such groups can play a significant direct or indirect role in healing past hurts. Directly, some groups engage in a healing ministry. Indirectly, a warmly supportive community is often the catalyst an individual needs to begin to examine past transgressions or emotional conflicts. The person may seek another member in the community with whom to share a situation and its effects. The very act of sharing past hurts—even with one person—in the context of a warm and accepting community can be tremendously transforming, and can enable the person to leave such pain behind.

Christian communities often are centered on the sacramental life. This is very true of Catholicism, which centers in the sacraments, especially the eucharist, where we believe Christ is truly present.

Sacramental celebrations bring the community together specifically to pray. The seven sacraments bridge the entire cycle of life and seek to make life and its major events holy. They give our lives back to God not in isolation but communally, and are a privileged place where God speaks to us. We will mention briefly the sacraments of baptism and the eucharist.

Baptism is the initial sacramental welcome of individuals into the church. It is both a family and community event. Here the person, adult or child, is immersed in the death and resurrection of Christ. The Holy Spirit transforms our inner life and makes us one with Christ and his community. This initiation sets the stage for our dyings and risings throughout life—our "letting go's" and our "transformations." It is the formal beginning of our life in Christ and his community. This initiation enables our participation in the sacramental and spiritual life of the church.

In the *eucharist* Christ speaks through the community gathered, through the sacred word of scripture and through the divine presence in the sacred body and blood. For me, this presence is occasionally almost tangible. I understand the word and feel the reality. Others report that Christ inspired them in their thanksgiving after communion, through the words of a hymn or the preaching of the word. I believe the mystery of Christ's presence for us and with us is most evident here. As with the early disciples on the road to Emmaus (Lk 24:13–35), we come to know the resurrected Jesus in the breaking of the bread. Such moments can be positively transformative if we are open to them.

The image of the *transfiguration* stands out as one of great importance in our quest for spiritual growth. Jesus was transfigured before the disciples and they saw him in glory. They encountered a deeper dimension, as we can too at the eucharist.

Prior to the Second Vatican Council (1962–1965), Catholics came to encounter God at *mass*. We might not have understood the Latin but we felt assured of God's presence. The mystery and transcendence of God came to the fore. Now, and quite rightly, the focus is more on the complementary roles of the priest and the ministers. Yet we must see them in the Spirit. That is, we need to see them transfigured in Christ, making his glory accessible to us in a different way than previously.

In a similar way we need to open ourselves to the transfigured glory of others in the church community. When we encounter some individuals, it might take quite a bit of doing for us to get beyond appearances to grace and truth. From others, Christ's goodness seems to radiate.

The priest's role, at its best, has always been to let others see Christ, to be a window to God in contrast to an articulator of rules. At the eucharist, he repeats Christ's words of institution, his words at his Last Supper with his disciples. In ministry, he seeks to show the loving service of Jesus washing the feet of his disciples.

The priest certainly must articulate rules and explain them clearly and their grounding in scripture and tradition. The temptation for the priest, and for other ministers as well, is to hide behind the rules, especially if they are rather introverted or unsure of themselves, rather than to see the rules as an opportunity to share Christ's love with others.

The church is a praying community. We gather for the sacraments regularly and also for retreats and spiritual conferences. We gather in various formats to pray in public in smaller groups (e.g., for the morning prayer of the church) and as a complete community for special occasions. Our life embraces both community and individual prayer. Prayer is key to sustaining and developing our moral life. Friends pray for one another; friendships energize community.

Time for Prayer

If we speak of our friendship with God embodied in our life of communal and personal prayer, we might also consider some practicalities surrounding this friendship. Primarily, like all friendships, our's with God *takes time.* There is no substitute for it. We may be able to take short times during the day to pray in the presence of God. But ultimately there is no substitute for having a somewhat regular prayer time and sticking to it. The issue here is one of priority. Our friendship with God and our spiritual progress require a personal investment. It is a challenge to give our relationship with Christ some prime time when there are so many other demands. And this may be particularly true when we are unsure of the demands that God may make of us in turn. Friendships are that way: They lead us where we might prefer not to go. Yet they make us most happy.

God is slow. I have found this in relating to God over the years. Since I am more in a hurry, I find this a little disconcerting. Just as Israel waited for centuries for God's plan to unfold, so too we must wait and learn patience. God's ultimate timing is superb, but it can throw our's off. Or, more precisely, it can lead to a more contemplative attitude. Not everything needs to be done quickly. The most substantive things in life are accomplished slowly. Character builds gradually just as we learn to speak a language one word or phrase at a time. The pace is slow but constant. God speaks through the Spirit and enables us to learn the next word.

Giving Ourselves Completely

Ultimately, we enter completely into our relationships with others and with God. We are to give all of ourselves. People report that as they grow in the life of prayer, they turn their activities more and more into prayerful moments. Short prayers characterize their day. They are increasingly with God in their spare moments.

Yet at times we feel as if we have nothing more to give. Again the poet Jessica Powers reminds us:

> No gift is proper to a Deity;
> no fruit is worthy for such power to bless.
> If you have nothing, gather back your sigh,
> and with your hands held high, your heart held high,
> lift up your emptiness![10]

Even when there is no *thing* to give, there is always *someone* to give—ourselves. Our giving manifests itself in living the life of virtue. This is an integrated life.

Ultimately we are called *to give everything to God.* For me, this was an early realization. At age nineteen, sitting in the back of a class on St. Francis de Sales' *Introduction to a Devout Life,* I realized quite clearly that everything was to be given to God. What I didn't realize was that this was a lifetime's task, a continual turning over, not just a once-and-for-all commitment.

The giving over of our lives to God is an ongoing process that does not occur in isolation. It is profoundly interpersonal and deeply personal. We grow together with our spiritual friends. Thus we turn in the following chapter once again to the role of friendship in our lives.

QUESTIONS FOR REFLECTION AND DISCUSSION

1. How does God speak to you? Are there other ways in which God speaks to you in addition to those we have mentioned above? Are there avenues of conversation that could be opened?

2. How do you pray now? Is prayer for you more of an individual or a communal reality?

3. How do you make time for prayer? How could you make time for prayer?

VI. Spiritual Friendships

$\mathcal{F}$riendship can change our lives. Good friends can lead us to maturity. Spiritual friends can help us become holy. Our relationships help us set the direction for our lives. In this chapter, we will speak of these relationships in more detail, especially the type of friendship referred to as spiritual direction.

Spiritual friendships vary in depth. Often, we have friendships in which occasionally we share spiritual topics but generally stay focused on the task at hand or the project to be accomplished.

There is the special friend we turn to in a crisis or spiritual need. I serve in this capacity for some friends. When his young grandson was facing life-threatening surgery, an old friend called and asked if I could come to pray with the family at the hospital. This crisis gave us an opportunity to reconnect the strands of our lives, which had been separated through circumstance.

Another level of friendship is that of our small group, which meets to pray and share faith. This is a more regular type of sharing—varying from once a week to once a month. Usually, in small groups there is a spiritual focus and a level of trust that enable the friends to open their spiritual lives to one another in some depth. Not only do these groups allow us to befriend ourselves, but they directly point us toward God. Here a friend might ask: "How is God speaking to you in your life?"—the kind of question that always gets us thinking. The example of the other group members who are struggling to live the gospel message is encouraging and can be a profound way of learning about the concrete living of the spiritual life today.

At times in our lives, we might have one or two friends with whom we can open our hearts most deeply. They are a real gift. To have a kindred spirit who understands us "backward and forward" and with whom we can communicate our daily successes, failures, anxieties and prayers is a special treasure. These relationships seem to develop over time and have a particular focus on spiritual growth, our progress in the virtuous life. Depth of prayer and personal commitment characterize such relationships, which are exemplified in the saints but are not uncommon today. For example, some married couples have this depth of spiritual relationship that transfigures them and the environment around them. One couple I know, notwithstanding having a large family, has such a depth of love and commitment that they take in preteenage children from dysfunctional families to love them back to wholeness. The fruit of their spiritual commitment to one another is in loving deeds of service to those in desperate need.

The Ministry of Spiritual Direction

Those who are seeking spiritual growth sometimes feel called by God to embrace that particular form of spiritual friendship referred to traditionally as spiritual direction. Currently, this type of spiritual friendship is experiencing a rapid expansion. A great deal of literature is being written on the spiritual director, sometimes referred to as the soul friend, and the process of direction. Many Christians are seeking this ongoing spiritual guidance.

Varying definitions of spiritual direction exist. A good one is that of theologian Sandra Schneiders:

> Spiritual Direction could be defined as a process carried out in the context of a one-to-one relationship in which a competent guide helps a fellow Christian to grow in the spiritual life by means of personal encounters that have the directee's spiritual growth as their explicit object.[1]

The director is most often a more mature and knowledgeable Christian who meets regularly with his or her friend, often referred to as the directee. The purpose of the meetings is the spiritual growth of the friend. A long tradition of this kind of spiritual direction pays attention to a person's experience of God and helps the "Christian to discern what in his or her experience is of God and what is not of God."[2] The relationship is an aid to us in listening to God speak and in figuring out how best to respond.

The director helps a person become aware of God and of the work of God in his or her life. As noted in an earlier chapter, we can be almost oblivious to our own patterns, which was made apparent to me once by a friend who had asked me to be his director. In sharing his life story, he noted how years ago he had left the seminary after a week's reflection. More recently, he had changed jobs within a day. (Luckily he had the competence to do such a thing!) I asked him if he thought he had a pattern of rapid decision making. He seemed puzzled by the question. Yet eventually he realized that he made major life decisions on impulse rather than in a thorough process of discernment. His emotions were very strong and kept him from taking the time to listen to God and respond more thoughtfully.

The Role of the Director

The action of the Holy Spirit is the basis for spiritual direction. In actuality, the director is helping the spiritual friend to be sensitive to the guidance of the Spirit and to remove any interior or exterior obstacles to that guidance. The soul friend tries to help the directee to be more free to respond.

This type of direction requires a certain type of spiritual maturity. Kenneth Leech believes that:

> I stand by my insistence in 1977 that spiritual direction is not essentially a ministry for specialists and professionals, but part of the ordinary pastoral ministry of every parish and every Christian community. Even more so do I stand by my suggestions that the role of "training" is extremely limited, and that this ministry is essentially a by-product of a life of prayer and growth in holiness.[3]

Leech's view certainly agrees with a lengthy Catholic tradition dating back to the monks in the desert. He argues against the extensive training some consider necessary for this ministry.

I believe that Leech is correct in stressing that personal holiness and one's own living in the Spirit are necessities in this ministry. We should avoid the tendency to want to overprofessionalize ministry. Much spiritual guidance occurs rather informally in our spiritual friendships. Here, good judgment and common sense prevail and can be quite helpful.

But to befriend a directee at a consistent and deeper level, I believe that some professional training is necessary. Spiritual direction often is educative. The director helps someone who is beginning the spiritual journey to get started. This requires some basic knowledge on the director's part, such as an awareness of the different ways that people begin the spiritual journey. On the other hand, a director will occasionally deal with a person who seems to be having special spiritual experiences. Here, in order to help the person discern the validity and meaning of such experiences, some knowledge is necessary of the higher levels of the life of prayer.

A knowledge of spiritual theology is necessary in these instances as is broader background in theology as the directee progresses in the spiritual life and begins to ask questions and express concerns. For example, often the question of the meaning of suffering will arise. Or the directee might ask about the role of the sacraments in spiritual growth. Such questions require a more detailed knowledge of theology and of church teaching.

A key point to keep in mind is that insofar as spiritual direction is a ministry, it represents the church community. Directors bring to it the wisdom of the community that must be learned both through study and experience. The teaching of the church is a mainstay in making correct discernments about God's work in our lives. It helps to balance the perils of subjectivism in making our decisions.

St. Francis de Sales believed that a director should be filled with "charity, learning and prudence."[4] If any of these three qualities is lacking, danger lurks. Good directors can be hard to find. Not all priests or religious sisters and brothers are comfortable in this ministry. However, there are increasing numbers of qualified lay directors who are active and effective. If we believe that we are called to this type of friendship, we have to make an initial judgment as to the qualities we are seeking and the availability of a director with these qualities. Often, our spiritual friends and the members of our communities of faith can help us in finding such a director.

The ministry calls for certain other qualities in the ministering person. Prime among them is warmth and empathy. Francis de Sales showed these in his ministry of direction. After giving over the relationship wholly to God,

> Then he entered fully into the relationship, calling upon his rich affective reserves, his empathy and his capacity for meaningful human interaction to see him through.[5]

Such human warmth helps to free the directee to share his or her innermost preoccupations and to respond most effectively to God's call.

> ...it is through being deeply known and accepted that we can know and accept ourselves honestly—that is, humbly—and simply and lovingly. The goal of ...[the] presentation is such self-knowledge because all the great spiritual teachers declare that self-knowledge is the foundation of contemplative life and love, no matter what our ministry or particular vocation.[6]

This is the great advantage of spiritual friendship. Friends facilitate our spiritual growth. The director or other spiritual friend can't produce spiritual growth but can help us along the way. God's grace and the directee's choices are operative here. Others can only be encouraging and support development.

A good director encourages and enlightens. He or she serves as a sounding board. It is often difficult for us to listen to our experience because we are not used to doing so and because we are preoccupied with other things. Though we must ultimately take responsibility for our own responses, it helps us to have a friend to give an account to. It is equally difficult to find a friend to listen with us to our experience as revealing God.

The Relevance of Psychological Models

A current concern in ministry these days is the benefit and limits of psychology in spiritual direction. A person's psychological and spiritual growth are intertwined but they are not identical.

A major question is the role of psychological models in direction. The "importation" of therapeutic ideas into direction has become prominent. We can read a great deal of literature about Jungian personality types as they affect our spiritual growth, or about the importance of paying attention to our feelings, or about the need for nonjudgmentalism in the one-to-one meeting. All these elements have their proper place. In excess, however, they can reflect the self-preoccupation of our culture rather than an exploration of the work of the Holy Spirit within us in order to reach out to our neighbor. Some concern exists that such direction can wind up, inadvertently to be sure, as tenuously Christian, having little to do with the central mysteries of faith, the demands of the moral life and the spiritual teaching of the Christian tradition. Growth in holiness calls for a proper balance of these concerns with a focus on listening to God and responding to God's call in our lives.

Concerns of Direction

The questions of concern in spiritual direction are as broad as human experience and as deep as the mystery of God. These aspects cannot be delineated in any complete fashion here, but we will mention a few critical elements so as to flesh out our description of this special type of friendship.

The director can help a person in *telling his or her life story*. Many direction relationships begin with a review of one's spiritual journey up to this point in life. This is of particular importance in mid-life when people tend to look back at their lives to search for meaning or for healing. Here we can have a moment of deeper conversion to Christ as we see in a clearer light the broad panorama of life.

A second important element in direction is discernment. The director frequently helps the friend *to discern God's call* and sometimes needs to clarify for the directee the criteria for discernment in the Christian tradition. The director should be concerned with the actual experience of the person and not what he or she thinks should be happening. The director needs to listen to the directee attentively and with the heart. He or she also may need to help a person distinguish the inner movement of the Spirit from other interior inclinations or feelings that point in different directions.

A director can also *help a person in a moment of crisis,* which can be an opportunity for deeper spiritual growth, of identification with Christ on the Cross, rather than a time of despair. The crisis may be brought on by external circumstances such as job loss or the death of a loved one. Or it may be an interior crisis of darkness in prayer, which is sometimes an indication of an internal blockage to the transfiguring power of grace. Just speaking to a friend about such moments can be part of the process of growth and healing that leads ultimately to action. The proof of our love for Christ and neighbor is in loving deeds. As one contemporary theologian notes:

> ...the currently assumed "measure" of spiritual growth tends to be far too introspective. True Christian spiritual growth points to the constant sharing of faith through some form of mission and ministry.[7]

Ultimately, as we grow toward spiritual maturity, we are called to give ourselves away completely to others in imitation of Christ.

QUESTIONS FOR REFLECTION AND DISCUSSION

1. Have you experienced spiritual friendship/direction as defined in this chapter? How did this relationship contribute to your spiritual growth?

2. How do you go about discerning God's call(s) in your life?

VII. When Relationships Falter: Sin, Healing and Reconciliation

Some time ago, I heard a sad story. The marriage of a couple I know, whose wedding I witnessed with high hopes, was headed toward divorce. Their friendship had failed. The news made me sad—actually a little depressed. You probably know, as I do, other couples in similar situations. What happened?

We have been speaking about the success of friendship with self, others and God over the last several chapters. We believe that these relationships are the impetus, the driving force, for spiritual and moral growth. As realists, however, we know that life is complex and relationships not only succeed but also falter or fail. All of us have a list of former friends tucked in the back of our heads. With some, the relationship ended on a sour or ugly note. Memories of these relationships and emotions may need to be healed. This chapter will concern itself with the healing that we all require at times.[1]

Healing occurs within the individual, in our interpersonal relationships and in our friendship with God. Sometimes it embraces self, neighbor and God all at once. For example, in a mother's seeking forgiveness from her teenage son for an unwarranted outburst, she not only affirms her relationship with him but also comes to a deeper, personal peace and accepts Christ's healing love.

76

The friendship dimensions of her life come together in this act of healing love.

Dimensions of the Healing Process

The stresses and strains of our day-to-day relationships offer ample opportunities for healing. One friend of mine wrote: "In my relationships, I have been thoughtless, unforgiving, and hurtful, quick with a sarcastic comment or critical glance." Many of us recognize ourselves in such comments and know that acting accordingly will lead to the dissolution of our interpersonal relationships. Here a sincere apology, a request for forgiveness, a direct conversation and a resolution to do better are necessary to keep the tear in our friendship from becoming a break.

At times, our relational stresses will cause us to look at our internal patterns. Why do we give those critical looks; from whom did we learn them? Do our sarcastic comments reflect our conversation with ourselves—our internal talk? We can learn new ways of speaking to ourselves and others but often it is not easy. Our habitual ways of thinking and speaking can be unyielding to untold numbers of good resolutions. Yet, healing grace can help us to let go of our self-defeating ways.

Stressed, failing or failed friendships offer a host of examples of situations that need healing. We will mention just a few aspects of friendship that may call for God's healing presence.

Expressing Our Anger

One of the important aspects of being human is being emotional. Often when we reflect on a failed relationship, we are conscious of strong emotions related to the dissolution even if this happened many years ago. One key emotion is *anger.*

> ...throughout our lives, we invest ourselves and suffer loss. The automatic response to any of these experiences is a feeling of hurt, which is rapidly transformed into anger.[2]

Anger is not a socially acceptable emotion. Sometimes we have trouble acknowledging that we are in fact angry. We have trouble acknowledging our loss. Often when we recognize our anger, we are not sure whether or how to express it because anger can destroy our relationships with others or with God. But unexpressed anger and hostility can destroy us as well:

> Stored anger eventually destroys the vitality of the person and is the source of "victim" behavior. The victim basically believes that he or she cannot do anything to rectify or change either self or situation. Learned helplessness results; the person takes no responsibility for his or her passive response.[3]

Some form of appropriate expression of anger is preferable.

If we express our anger, we may do so in ways that are destructive of others, either verbally or physically. A sister friend wrote recently that *"home is where the violence is...."*[4] Not only are children the victims of violence in dysfunctional families but, she laments, they often are returned quickly by law to the same abusive situation. The sad thing is that violence can be acted out in cycles. Our anger can express itself again and again in aggression and violence.

We can also express anger nonviolently but inappropriately toward a person who is less threatening than the one who has questioned our integrity or self-esteem. The classic case, not infrequent these days, is "taking out" the angers of the workplace on someone else, perhaps a spouse or a child. Anger from one relationship can be displaced into another. We all too frequently do this to the people we love the most.

The key to dealing with our anger effectively is not to bury it or express it violently or deflect it on others but to seek to express it constructively. We must make some choices about our feelings and how best to respond to others.

One author suggests eight helpful steps for dealing with anger:

1. I release the energy of my anger in an active physical way (walking, swimming…) or in a more passive way (reading a book…).
2. I take time to get in touch with my feeling of anger and reflect on its source.
3. I think about the anger's ramifications if it is left unattended.
4. I choose to discuss my feelings with a third party, or to write about them, in order to clarify them in my mind.
5. I reflect on my hope for the outcome.
6. I acknowledge that I own my feelings, and I avoid blaming the other for my anger.
7. I find a mutually convenient time and place to speak with the other person.
8. I choose to change my own response if the situation is nonreconcilable.[5]

At the conclusion of the process we may act, as in Step 7, or realize that nothing can be done and choose to accept this. Dealing with our anger involves coming to terms with the reality of a situation and of the people we deal with, not a partial view of them. Then we must move on.

...emotional forgiving comes only after substantial time and energy have been devoted to forgiving in the intellectual arena. Getting in touch with the source of anger is a painful process.[6]

Our deep anger from childhood or early life—anger more related to an ongoing situation rather than a single incident—may take an extended period of time to heal. Such inner hostility needs healing if our present friendships are to be fruitful.

A man I knew once shared with a group on retreat how he left home in anger at eighteen and joined the Marines. Years later he wished he had reconciled with his dad before the man died. He then placed the resolution in God's hands and moved on to do constructive things in his life, such as giving retreats.

Suffering in Relationships

One author compared the inner process of recognition and healing to Jacob's wrestling with the angel in the Old Testament:

> And we know the story. The angel of the Lord comes and wrestles with Jacob all night. On his part, Jacob lets himself confront his own fears head on, in a raging battle. He summons every ounce of courage he can; every drop of sweat is measured with only one purpose in mind: to come to really know himself, to know his call, to know his God. And Jacob wins...[but] Jacob bears for eternity the scar of self-discovery.[7]

Just as in Jacob's wrestling with the angel, dealing with inner emotions can leave residual scars that stay with us. Years later we may get angry all over again in recalling an incident of hurt. This may pass quickly but it reminds us that there is a scar.

No one escapes the scars and suffering of life. Our friendship with self, others and God is tremendously liberating and propels our spiritual growth. But in this life none of these is perfect. Every person bears some interior damage from relationships gone bad. Even the best of friendships is not without its rough spots and discord. We don't always communicate well with each other; we become preoccupied with self; we cause pain to our friend. Not only this, but we repeat our conflicts at regular intervals. We may have a major disagreement or fight with a friend at least every month and can't seem to stay on an even keel.

This suffering enters our friendship with God as well. At times we can't hear God speaking and we don't feel like listening or praying. This may be our own laziness or it could be the "dark night of the soul" that St. John of the Cross discusses. God seems distant and we are lost in the blackness of the spiritual universe. Often these symptoms indicate that something in us is blocking our communication with God and we need to let it go. As we grow spiritually, this process does not get any easier. My own experience is that knowing this has to happen, and even writing about letting go, makes it no easier in practice to accept the suffering and purification inherent in a prayerful friendship with God. Jesus warned us that we would have to take up our Cross, and he gave the example.

Alienation from God

Not only do we need to accept suffering as part of ourselves and our relationships, we also need to acknowledge our alienation from self, others and God. *We have sinned* and we need to accept responsibility for our sin and its effects.

Sin can be seen as a failure to respond in love to God. Sin is "...an out-and-out rejection of God's summons to a life centered on love,..., and truth, and in its stead, the sign of a life centered on manipulation, domination and deception."[8] Instead of acting in such a way as to enhance our relations and move toward the heavenly reign, we do the opposite. We exploit and manipulate others, as can be seen in business dealings where we shade the truth (i.e., lie) to investors to enhance our profit.

Our sin can reach beyond us and assume its own reality. Once it happens, it can have long-term effects that we can't take back. Sin remains in the world, in our parish and civic communities. We see this, for example, in the Middle East where people have worked for decades to try to heal ancient hurts and are only now having some little success. No one even knows how these conflicts began, as they have been so long lasting. Closer to home we see the social effects of sin in the racism that is passed on from one generation to the next, by word and example. Sin can destroy our communities and our friendships. No one is completely free of sin and its effects.

Healing and Reconciliation[9]

It is no wonder that many of us are concerned with personal healing and reconciliation. The failure of marriages, other relationships, and our own sinfulness and sorrow lead us to the Christian community for solace, a tradition rich in opportunities for healing. Some involve the search for physical healing; many more concern the search for peace of mind. Services and masses for healing are quite popular these days.

In the healing process, we are in great need of the mercy of God. We rely completely upon it and without it will not be healed. Yet God's grace, even with our utmost cooperation, often works slowly. We live a process of being healed, which takes time and may never be complete "'til heaven." We may find more opportunities of letting go of past hurts and sins as new experiences in life make us conscious of hidden dimensions of past situations.

Healing in our church and in our ministry for the church is a multifaceted reality that comes in a variety of ways. Many of us have been healed in *reading the word of God in scripture*. Sometimes it just seems that a reading from the bible or a scriptural reference in our daily prayers almost leaps off the page as it speaks to an important situation in our lives. While we might not say that this is the meaning of the passage in a critical sense, we know that God has spoken and we are healed. And propelled forward!

Prayer, if we can pray, is often a time for healing to take place. Whether in our rote prayers such as the "Our Father" ("forgive us our trespasses") or in our spontaneous prayers in God's presence, we can experience a deep reconciliation with God and our neighbor. This takes some acknowledgment of what is going on in our lives rather than denial. One friend avoids taking time for private prayer when she knows she has something negative or sinful to talk over with Jesus but doesn't want to!

Prayer need not be just personal. We may ask others to pray with us and for us. This can be in a public setting such as a healing service or in a group that prays for healing of memories, but it also can be more private. Often we can ask someone to pray with us. I know people who even call their spiritual friends and pray together over the telephone for themselves or for situations that need God's healing touch.

The *eucharist,* as the central prayer of the Catholic community, is a sign of God's great love for us and a celebration of ongoing healing and reconciliation. It is a time of closeness to God when we focus on his presence and let it transform us. Through Christ's power the ravages of sin can be transformed as we ask for forgiveness. Here the community is joined as we listen to the word, share the bread of life, pray for one another's needs and offer each other a sign of peace. If we can get beyond the familiarity (not always easy), we can be deeply touched by the power of the Spirit healing here. Thus we can be energized to be a healing presence to others in the wider community.

In reaching out to others, we can often serve as a *spiritual friend.* We all need this kind of friendship ourselves for our own spiritual growth. To get to the roots of our sinfulness and distress, we need help. The merciful presence of God is often mediated to us by others. When we are that other, it can be a humbling experience as we recognize our own inadequacies and sinfulness. Yet it is a profound form of service.

Often we are the last to see the patterns in our own lives. One service a spiritual friend can render is to listen; a second is to gently point out those patterns of life, of sin, or of relationship that seem to be destructive or self-defeating. A spiritual friend can help with discernment and be supportive.

We live a *process* of being saved. Deep emotions that flare up and burn brightly often need to be worked on over extended periods of time before the healing process takes hold. We as spiritual friends cannot rush the process, although we can help to point efforts in the right direction. Emotions unacknowledged in prayer and in word can continue to be destructive. Patient support can work wonders as our friend struggles. At these times, we can point out that the willing and free choice of how to act determines moral responsibility—not our feelings. A little knowledge and a sympathetic ear can be the instruments of God's reconciling love in such situations.

Just as contemporary psychology speaks of stages of growth throughout life, so too the great spiritual authors such as St. Francis de Sales speak of stages of loving, of growth in the Spirit. From our own lives, we can see that the roots of sin in us take time to become obvious and to be dealt with. We struggle with the limits of our gifts and our personalities. As we grow spiritually, it seems that our vision becomes clearer and we develop a deeper sensitivity of soul. Our need for reconciliation and healing thus becomes even more obvious.

The *sacrament of reconciliation* is a primary means of healing in the Catholic community. While the frequency of its use is down, its power is unabated. It is a sacrament worthy of serious preparation and can have profound effects. As one who has experienced the sacrament from "both sides," I can testify that I have found it to be a healing experience for me. And a number of those who have come to me as minister of the sacrament have reported that they too have been healed. This has been startling to me! The power of God in this sacrament can heal the deepest roots and fissures of sin and give ongoing strength and power for the journey. Here is a time to confess and let go of the results of sin.

Our sins impact us as well as others. Perhaps the people we have hurt have disappeared from our lives never to be heard from again. The sacrament provides an opportunity to take those we've harmed and past events and turn them over to the Lord, realizing that God's love can bring good out of evil.

The sacrament of reconciliation brings us face-to-face with the reality that we are not perfect and never will be. We are pilgrims and will always have our struggles. The sacrament, especially in its face-to-face format, provides an opportunity to share a bit of one's life story and to ask a few questions. For some individuals, this may be the only real opportunity they have to share or to ask important questions. Of course, their ability to do so will be affected by the openness of the confessor and the time frame of the confession. Sometimes an appointment with a confessor is called for; this will give both priest and penitent time to share their thoughts.

The sacrament of reconciliation can be a powerful spiritual experience. I have found myself saying things to the person in the confessional situation that I have not thought of in years. Occasionally, startling coincidences, such as randomly reading a theological article that within the space of a few hours provides the answer to a person's serious question, have left me conscious that divine providence is operative. It is God's power that heals.

The ministry of healing in the church is certainly a multi-faceted one. Scripture reading, prayer, the eucharist, spiritual friendship and the sacrament of reconciliation, among others, are special occasions for the personal healing that is so much sought in our contemporary world.

Through the healing process we can begin over again. There is no time when we cannot start afresh. Our life is hope-filled. We release past and present parts of our lives in hope for the future. Our trust rests in God to whom we give the past with its sins, hurts and mistakes.

QUESTIONS FOR REFLECTION AND DISCUSSION

1. Why do some friendships persist and others fail?

2. Could you name a relationship of yours that has

failed? What caused the breakdown? Have others helped you in the healing process?

3. Have you experienced healing in ways other than those mentioned in this chapter?

4. Have you ever been an agent for the healing of others? What did you do?

VIII. The Virtuous Life: Living in Response to God's Grace[1]

Twenty years ago I remember going to a large prayer meeting and seeing many people who had met Jesus in a new way. They had opened up to God's love and were filled with enthusiasm. One person familiar with the group pointed out a man and noted that he had suffered from mental illness for a number of years, but in the warm and accepting environment of the prayer meeting he was growing spiritually and returning to health. I noticed that this atmosphere, which focused on Christ and communal support, enabled people to risk forming relationships with one another that they would have been reluctant to risk in the past. Their deeper conversion freed them for personal spiritual growth.

The healing we spoke of in the previous chapter is a continuing element in the conversion process. As we work our way through life, we continually encounter areas of ourselves and our relationships that need to be healed. The healing frees us for further growth, which in turn makes us aware of additional need for healing. This dynamic of grace seems to go on throughout life.

Growth in Virtue

The complementary dynamic of the spiritual life is our growth in virtue.

> Most would accept the idea that a virtue is a disposition to act, desire, and feel that involves the exercise of judgment and leads to a recognizable human excellence, an instance of human flourishing.[2]

We can always form our character more completely by our loving deeds and be converted to Christ more deeply. Of course, by the time we realize this, we are already adults. We have made some important decisions; we have taken in, wittingly or unwittingly, a host of influences from parents, family members, neighbors, teachers, the media and others. We have formed ourselves and been formed in a number of ways. The question is: What do we do now? Where do we go from here? Our contention is that a move toward spiritual depth in the virtue of charity is the best possible direction we can take.

Living the virtues is the positive side of the Christian moral life. In our litigious society, we hear much about the law. And we in the church certainly respect the law as expressed, for example, in the Ten Commandments. But the law is often the minimum. It provides the boundaries within which we operate. And while we all need boundaries at times, they are not the essence of the moral life, which is about doing good, living virtuously and thus growing spiritually. It involves making responsible decisions about who to become and what to do in the light of Christ's love and example.

In living the virtuous life and not outside of it we are happy and at peace. Contentment is not in having something, such as a prize or a house, but in being someone—a person living the life of charity.

Growth in virtue is never complete. We can always live more fully the life of charity with its attendant self-discipline. There are always areas of our thinking and doing that need some letting go of the past and transformation in the light of Christ.

> …the path toward virtue must be a never ending quest, not a possession. As travelers toward a fulfillment not yet given we must find some way to come to terms with this sense that we are "on the way." Two false answers to this experience are often given: We may *doubt* that any fulfillment is possible; or we may seek a calm *certainty of possession*, an assurance that we have reached the goal.[3]

Basically we need to release absolute control—actually in practice we still maintain quite a bit of it—and accept our need for God. Without God's grace we can do nothing; without our work, grace is ineffectual. Our freedom is ultimate. We can accept or reject God's life. Our freedom is limited. We need God's help.

Living the virtuous life consistently is a gift of God's grace. After we've made our good resolutions a million times and failed, we begin to realize that we need God's help. Charity is a gift with which we need to work. But ultimately all is in God's hands, and we respond to God's gift to us. We listen to God's word and respond with our lives.

With grace, we can develop the virtues throughout life. The personal encounters and friendships, the special and lesser events, the spiritual experiences of seeing and listening are always prodding us to growth. We are continually being called out of ourselves to generous and self-sacrificing love for others. Paradoxically, this brings us our deepest fulfillment this side of heaven.

Our lives are shaped by our vision and priorities. If we are moving toward a goal, we make our decisions in this light. These decisions form us, and in a sense we can say that our goals form us. A friend who has decided to make his family the priority declines invitations to do many other things in order to go to soccer games and spend some time with his growing children. He is forming himself primarily as a father rather than as a community or church volunteer, for example—though he may choose to do these good things when his children are grown.

The virtues we need to practice vary throughout our lives and reflect our priorities. *Patience* comes to the fore in bringing up children, and *patience with ourselves* is important in senior years. Our vocational *commitment* to marriage, the single life or the priesthood may be tested at another time. Our *generosity* in serving others may be called on in community service or care for the infirm.

The virtues we exemplify may also be a matter of temperament. Some of us are more attuned to civility or gentleness; others are inclined to justice or advocacy for the poor. These "natural virtues" enable us to build on our strengths as we grow spiritually.

God may call us to the practice of certain virtues—even to those we don't like—through life circumstances. Or God may speak to us more directly, in prayer. A friend recently felt the call to simplify her life, letting go of some involvements and possessions in order to focus more time on prayer and a particular ministry. Others of us, including myself, thought that we were embracing a life of gospel poverty and freedom of concern for material goods and wound up spending large amounts of time examining budgets and raising money. God's call to spiritual growth can be both mysterious and challenging and outside our plans and expectations.

Donald Capps argues that certain virtues are most important at different points of the life cycle. Using the framework of Erik Erikson's eight psychosocial stages of growth through the life cycle, he contends that:

> ...even as we are disposed toward certain sins at given stages of the life cycle, we are also disposed toward certain virtues. In contrast to the deadly sins, these virtues...orient us toward life in ways that enhance human community of every kind, enable us to discern God's intentions for the world and to contribute to their realization, and contribute to our personal well-being in its various interrelated aspects.[4]

These virtues stretch from the hope, will and courage of early life through the care and wisdom of middle and late adulthood. The disposition to virtue, while an inherent capacity, can be cultivated individually and in the community.

Our practice of individual virtues involves our emotions. When we are at our best, our thoughts and feelings are integrated. But as J. Budziszewski remarks in his work, we are often only half-done. The "proto-virtues," as he calls them, are the way stations en route to true excellence,[5] and are often what we practice here and now. We operate out of some admixture of duty and charity. In some aspects of our lives, our thoughts and feelings are at one; in other aspects, they are headed in different directions. We can be at peace, conflicted or somewhere in between. I may know that the loving thing to do is to help my brother move to a new apartment, but I feel like staying in bed that Saturday morning. This may be momentary. Other dissonances of thought and feeling may be more deep seated. For example, I may know intellectually that God loves me but feel that God is always angry with me for my mistakes.

At best, we align ourselves with the truth of our own human dignity and that of others. We seek to form our thoughts and feelings according to the gospel. The ideal is a holy integration.

Friendships and Communities

How does this virtuous life, this life lived in charity, develop? Essentially, it grows or diminishes in relationships with others, which we have discussed already at some length. We are certainly products of our families. As adults we can see our parents' influence in our patterns of living and relating to others. We may have learned discipline, nonviolence, respect for others or the opposite. Our growth in virtue can be in following or reversing what we have learned.

The virtuous life grows in a community. The presence, example and actions of others can help us move forward. Local communities help pull us out of our self-preoccupation into a concern for others. Members of communities provide living examples of integrity, honesty, justice and the other virtues. They challenge us to add our particular gifts. In community, we learn that some of us have more difficulty than others with particular virtues. And all of us have difficulty in persistently doing the good. Parish communities at their best exemplify the full range of virtues and the mutuality that makes for spiritual growth.

Within this community context, we develop those personal spiritual friendships that are the key to our progress. Trusted friends can teach us, challenge us and support us. At their best, friends grow more and more in friendship with God and show this in generous service to others in the community. This charity spreads and touches other members of the community—indeed, it touches the world. The work of some of the great spiritual friends in the church (e.g., St. Francis de Sales and St. Jane de Chantal) continues to have an influence down to the present day.

Virtues grow in relationships, and relationships flourish in communities. We need communities in order to grow, in particular, religious communities such as parishes or prayer groups.

> The scriptural character of religious community shapes individual character. Knowing the stories of the faith of Abraham or the love of John shapes people's own capacities to trust and to love. The story of the founding of a religious community becomes part of individual life-stories. As this happens, the convictions of the community become personal convictions.[6]

The wide religious community keeps us on track and challenges us to grow. Its role is essential to progress in living virtuously. In the community lives a man of such integrity and good judgment that we would always want to work for him, and a woman whose kindness and peace of heart are so radiant that we are warmed for the whole next day. Special people whom we meet live the virtues and raise the question "What kind of person does God want me to become?"

Recently, I saw a sign in front of a church in southern Virginia that said "Lite Worship" was at 9 a.m. on Sunday. Regular worship was at 11. Lite worship, it seems to me, makes for spiritual thinness. What we seek from our parish community is the weight of the stories, the prayer and the principles that propel us toward spiritual and moral growth, not the less filling variety.

While less fat and more meat may be significant for our spiritual growth, we are quick to realize that there is no shortcut to virtue. Patience, gentleness, humility, commitment, generosity and like virtues take time to develop. There is no easy way. We need to work continually; we need to seek God's help; we need the good example in the local congregation.

Charity Is the Central Virtue

Charity is the root and center of all the virtues that grow in friendship and community. The unity and integration of our thoughts and feelings and, ultimately, of our whole being is in this love. Charity nourishes all the individual virtues and is the river from which they flow.

Christian love, love in the Spirit of Jesus, presupposes our natural ability to love, which is always able to come to a deeper perfection through charity. Grace transforms our natural love or even supplies for it in some instances where its growth has been arrested.

> ...though the several levels of virtue form a continuous way, we may *experience* seemingly unbridgeable chasms along this way. We may experience a discontinuity so severe that it can even—as Pieper says in his discussion of love—seem akin to dying.[7]

It seems to me that as we grow in the spiritual life, we go from complexity to unity. The patience, humility, generosity and other virtues that we seek to develop earlier in life come to be seen more and more as aspects of love. This process involves turning everything to the good. As we grow in love we take every opportunity to serve. We look for ways to do good in the daily aspects of life. We seek to make the best of daily occurrences, difficult situations or the transitions in life. Growth in virtue goes on until death.

We form our character in action. The proof of a loving heart is in loving deeds. We need self-examination but not in excess. We need to balance necessary reflectiveness, which varies from person to person, with the action that focuses on others and their well-being and takes us out of ourselves. Christ is encountered in serving others.

Throughout our lives, we develop in this core or central virtue of charity. Francis de Sales gives a general description of this trajectory. His four stages of loving move from initial conversion to that complete love which is known to you and me occasionally and to the saints more frequently.

Joy Characterizes Holiness

Joy, God's gift to us, is the result of a virtuous life. It is nothing that society itself can manufacture and give to us. Joy is not pleasure, though sometimes the two are connected.

> It is illustrated in a saying a friend of mine learned from his grandmother. She taught him: The world is divided into givers and takers; the takers eat well and the givers sleep well....Joy comes from giving, sacrificing, trusting in God.[8]

Joy is intrinsic to the virtuous life. The rightly ordered life, moving in a positive direction, makes us happy on the surface and gives a deep inner contentment. This does not mean that suffering is nonexistent but, rather, that joy peeks through. St. Jane de Chantal, for example, even while struggling with doubts of faith over many years, was still a humorous and positive presence to the "recreation" of her sisters in their religious community. One biographer notes that they missed her good company when she was absent visiting other monasteries.[9] Joy can be copresent with suffering.

Joy comes from following Christ and embracing his teaching—both the cross and the resurrection. Ultimately, joy is in doing what God wants and not just what I want. Joy is the fruit of a meaningful life.

Our life of charity is Christ's life—an inner transformation in the Spirit and an outer transformation in the way we act. The good example of Christians points us toward their exemplar—Jesus. We seek to measure up to his level, not to level him down to ours.Our quest to be like him is unending.

QUESTIONS FOR REFLECTION AND DISCUSSION

1. What do you see as your characteristic virtue?

2. Have you experienced the inner joy of following Christ?

3. How do friendships work or fail within a broader community?

4. Has reading this book given you any insights that might help you to deepen your spiritual life?

Notes

I. THE WORLD TODAY

1. I wish to thank Mrs. Rowena Muller Morris for her contributions to this chapter.

2. William J. Doherty, *Soul Searching: Why Psychotherapy Must Promote Moral Responsibility* (New York: Basic Books, 1995), pp. 7–8.

3. See Gertrude Himmelfarb, *The De-Moralization of Society* (New York: Alfred A. Knopf, 1995), pp. 221–34.

4. Barbara Dafoe Whitehead, "Dan Quayle Was Right," *The Atlantic*, April, 1993, pp. 47–84.

5. Daniel Patrick Moynihan, "Defining Deviancy Down," *The American Scholar*, Winter, 1993.

6. Himmelfarb, pp. 11–12.

7. Robert N. Bellah et al., *Habits of the Heart* (New York: Harper and Row, 1985), p. 285.

8. Cited in Stephen R. Covey, A. Roger Merrill and Rebecca R. Merrill, *First Things First* (New York: Simon & Schuster, 1994), p. 114.

9. See Robert Wuthnow, *Sharing the Journey: Support Groups and America's New Quest for Community* (New York: Free Press, 1994).

10. Stephen R. Covey, *The 7 Habits of Highly Effective People* (New York: Simon & Schuster, 1989).

11. Ibid., p. 32.

12. William Bennett, *The Book of Virtues* (New York: Simon & Schuster, 1993).

13. Ibid., p. 11.

14. See my article "Commitment" in *Everyday Holiness* (De Sales School of Theology, 1994).

II. GROWING SPIRITUALLY

1. See Gilbert C. Meilaender, *The Theory and Practice of Virtue,* (Notre Dame: University of Notre Dame Press, 1984), pp. 1–44. The definition here comes from Josef Pieper, *The Four Cardinal Virtues* (Notre Dame: University of Notre Dame Press, 1966), p. xii.

2. Meilaender, p. 13.

3. Robert M. Hutchins, "Make It a Habit," *Commonweal*, April 21, 1995, p. 14.

4. Robert P. Maloney, "Listening as the Foundation for Spirituality," *Review for Religious* 51 (1992): 659–74.

5. Wendy M. Wright, "Fools for Christ," *Weavings* 9/6 (1994): 23–31.

6. Ibid., p. 30.

7. See William A. Barry, *Spiritual Direction and the Encounter with God* (New York: Paulist Press, 1992), pp. 72–73.

8. See Donald Nicholl, "Stop: Be Still," in *Holiness* (New York: Paulist Press, 1987), pp. 62–85.

9. This section draws on my earlier work "Progress in Our Spiritual Life: A Salesian View," which originally appeared in *Deacon Digest* (February, 1991).

10. St. Francis de Sales, *Treatise on the Love of God*, vol. II, trans. John K. Ryan (Rockford, IL: TAN Books, 1974), p. 86.

11. Stephen R. Covey et al., *First Things First* (New York: Simon & Schuster, 1994).

12. St. Francis de Sales, *Selected Letters*, trans. Elisabeth Stopp (New York: Harper & Bros., 1960), p. 59.

13. Hutchins, p. 15.

14. G. Simon Harak, *Virtuous Passions: The Formation of Christian Character* (New York: Paulist Press, 1993), p. 3.

15. Ibid., p. 23.

III. FRIENDSHIP WITH SELF

1. For much of what follows, see Isabel Anders, *The Faces of Friendship* (Cambridge, MA: Cowley, 1992), pp. 46–55.

2. Ibid., p. 50.

3. Eugene Kennedy, *On Being a Friend* (New York: Continuum, 1982), p. 60.

4. Janet Ruffing, "Resisting the Demon of Busyness," *Spiritual Life* 41/2 (Summer, 1995): 79–89.

5. Diane D. Gautney, "Discover Real Rest," *Spiritual Life* 41 (Spring, 1995): 4-11.

6. See Sheila Garcia, "Letting Go," *Spiritual Life* 39 (Summer, 1993): 91-95.

7. Ibid., p. 92.

IV. FRIENDSHIP WITH OTHERS

1. See St. Francis de Sales, *Introduction to the Devout Life*, abridged by Madame Yvonne Stephan, translated by Joseph D. Bowler, O.S.F.S., and Lewis S. Fiorelli, O.S.F.S. (Rockford, IL: TAN Books, 1990).

2. Ibid., p. 189.

3. Ibid., pp. 189–90.

4. Isabel Anders, *The Faces of Friendship* (Cambridge, MA: Cowley, 1992), p. 58.

5. Steve Donahue, "What Is Work Anyway?," *The Catholic Worker*, December, 1994, p. 5.

6. Anders, p. 73.

7. See Terrence J. Moran, C.SS.R., "Risking the Distance: Religious Men and Friendship," *America*, December 12, 1992, p. 468.

8. Melanie Phillips, "The 'Me' Generation," *The Tablet*, July 1, 1995, p. 832.

9. Mary Hunt as cited in Gilbert Meilaender, "Men and Women—Can We Be Friends?" *First Things* (May, 1993): 9.

10. Deborah Tannen as cited in Meilaender, p. 12.

11. Meilaender, p. 13.

12. Wendy M. Wright, "Refection on Spiritual Friendship Between Men and Women," *Weavings* II (July/August, 1987): 19.

13. Pope John Paul, "Letter to Women," *Origins* 25 (July 27, 1995): 3.

14. U.S. Catholic Conference, "Strengthening the Bonds of Peace," November, 1994.

15. Susan A. Ross and Mary Catherine Hilkert, O.P., "Feminist Theology: A Review of Literature," *Theological Studies* 56 (June, 1995): 327–52.

V. FRIENDSHIP WITH GOD

1. Paula Mullins, *Newsweek,* December 19, 1994, p. 12.

2. Isabel Anders, *The Faces of Friendship* (Cambridge, MA: Cowley, 1992), p. 10. Also see Wilkie Au, S.J., *By Way of the Heart: Toward a Holistic Christian Spirituality* (New York: Paulist Press, 1989), pp. 43–48.

3. Mitch Finley, "Male and Catholic in Confusing Times," *America,* September 26, 1992, p. 186.

4. For a more detailed discussion of scripture and tradition, see *The Development of Christian Character,* my sequel to this volume.

5. Jessica Powers, "This Trackless Solitude," as quoted in Robert Morneau, "The Spirituality of Jessica Powers," *Spiritual Life* 36 (1990): 152.

6. Michael Flecky, "Hopkins in Ireland," *America,* December 10, 1994, p. 16.

7. Paul J. Wadell, *Friendship and the Moral Life* (Notre Dame: University of Notre Dame Press, 1989), p. 140.

8. St. Francis de Sales, *Treatise on The Love of God* as quoted in Wendy M. Wright, *Francis de Sales* (New York: Crossroad, 1993), p. 144.

9. See the instruction on meditation offered by St. Francis de Sales in his *Introduction to the Devout Life,* abridged by Madame Yvonne Stephan, translated by Joseph D. Bowler, O.S.F.S., and Lewis S. Fiorelli, O.S.F.S. (Rockford, IL: TAN, 1990), pp. 60–72.

10. Jessica Powers, "If You Have Nothing," as quoted by Morneau, p. 155.

VI. SPIRITUAL FRIENDSHIPS

1. Sandra Schneiders, "The Contemporary Ministry of Spiritual Direction," in *Spiritual Direction: Contemporary Readings,* edited by Kevin G. Culligan, O.C.D. (Locust Valley, NY: Living Flame Press, 1983), p. 46.

2. William A. Barry, S.J., "Spiritual Direction: Recovery of a Tradition," *Warren Lecture Series, No. 30* (The University of Tulsa, March 20, 1994), p. 3.

3. Kenneth Leech, "Is Spiritual Direction Losing Its Bearings?" *The Tablet,* May 22, 1993, p. 634.

4. St. Francis de Sales, *Introduction to the Devout Life,* Part I, Chapter 4, abridged by Madame Yvonne Stephan, translated by Joseph D. Bowler, O.S.F.S., and Lewis S. Fiorelli, O.S.F.S. (Rockford, IL: TAN, 1990).

5. Wendy M. Wright, *Bond of Perfection* (New York: Paulist Press, 1985), p. 203.

6. Joann Wolski Conn, "A Developmental View of Salesian Spirituality," *Review for Religious* 52 (Jan.–Feb., 1993): 56–68.

7. Matthias Neuman, O.S.B., "Am I Growing Spiritually? Elements for a Theology of Growth" *Review for Religious* 42/1 (1983): 47.

VII. WHEN RELATIONSHIPS FALTER

1. A chapter in the companion volume to this one will discuss communal healing.

2. Brenda Hermann, M.S.B.T., "Anger Revisited," *Human Development* 11/2 (Summer, 1990): 15.

3. Ibid.

4. Sr. Josephine, "Home Is Where the Violence Is...," *Haven Notes* 1 (Spring, 1995): 1.

5. Hermann, p. 17.

6. Ibid.

7. John Allan Loftus, S.J., "Images of Healing," *Review for Religious* (May-June, 1989): 411.

8. James A. O'Donohoe, "Toward a Theology of Sin," *Church* 2/1 (Spring, 1986): 50.

9. This section originally appeared in *Deacon Digest* (August, 1991): 27–28.

VIII. THE VIRTUOUS LIFE

1. Some of the ideas in this chapter appeared originally in "How Do You Spell V-I-R-T-U-E?" published by the Catholic News Service in its *Faith Alive* series.

2. Lee H. Yearley, "Recent Work on Virtue," *Religious Studies Review* 16/1 (January, 1990): 2.

3. Gilbert Meilaender, *The Theory and Practice of Virtue* (Notre Dame: University of Notre Dame Press, 1984), p. 38.

4. Donald Capps, *Deadly Sins and Saving Virtues* (Philadelphia: Fortress Press, 1987).

5. J. Budziszewski, *The Resurrection of Nature: Political Theory and the Human Character* (Ithaca: Cornell University Press, 1986).

6. Craig Dykstra, "The Importance of Stories," *Initiatives in Religion* 2/2 (Spring, 1993): 1.

7. Meilaender, p. 35.

8. Milton F. Walsh, "To God, Who Gives Joy to My Youth," *America*, March 11, 1995, p. 31.

9. Elizabeth Stopp, *Madame De Chantal* (London: Faber and Faber, 1962).

Annotated Bibliography

Anders, Isabel. *The Faces of Friendship*. Cambridge, MA: Cowley, 1992.

> *Anders offers a practical and clearly written exposition on friendship in its many varieties.*

Francis de Sales, Jane de Chantal: Letters of Spiritual Direction. Selected and introduced by Wendy M. Wright and Joseph F. Power, O.S.F.S. New York: Paulist Press, 1988.

> *This work not only gives insight into spiritual direction but provides the best concise introduction to Salesian spiritual theology now available.*

Harak, G. Simon, S.J., *Virtuous Passions: The Formation of Christian Character*. New York: Paulist Press, 1993.

> *Harak's excellent work deals in some detail with our body and its passions. He presents current studies of our emotional life and links these to St. Thomas Aquinas' views on the passions and to the role of the passions in St. Ignatius Loyola's famous* Spiritual Exercises.

Kennedy, Eugene. *On Being a Friend*. New York: Continuum, 1982.

> *Kennedy's short chapters are filled with commonsense reflections on friendship.*

Kiesling, Christopher. *Celibacy, Prayer and Friendship.* New York: Alba House, 1978.
Kiesling offers a readable and practical discussion of celibacy and its necessary relationship to prayer and friendship.

Meilaender, Gilbert C. *The Theory and Practice of Virtue.* Notre Dame: University of Notre Dame Press, 1984.
Meilaender's essays offer a thoughtful introduction to virtue ethics from a Protestant point of view.

Porter, Jean. *The Recovery of Virtue: The Relevance of Aquinas for Christian Ethics.* Louisville: Westminster, 1990.
Porter gives an excellent contemporary theological exposition of St. Thomas Aquinas' theology of the virtues.

Sofield, Loughlan, and Juliano, Carroll. *Collaborative Ministry: Skills and Guidelines.* Notre Dame: Ave Maria Press, 1987.
In this short work, Sofield and Juliano cover many of the basic elements that make for effective collaboration in pastoral ministry today.

Wadell, Paul J. *Friendship and the Moral Life.* Notre Dame: University of Notre Dame Press, 1989.
Wadell argues for the importance of friendship to the moral life. His clearly written volume draws on Aristotle and St. Thomas Aquinas to show the importance of friendships with others and God for moral growth.

Wright, Wendy M. *Francis de Sales.* New York: Crossroad, 1993.
Wright's book offers selections from St. Francis De Sales' Introduction to the Devout Life *and his other major works with a contemporary reflection on each excerpt. This work is ideal for those who want an overview of St. Francis' major ideas with contemporary reflections.*

Index